brilliant

supply
teacher

Withdrawn from Stock

brilliant

supply
teacher

What you need to know to be a truly
outstanding teacher

Laurence French

Harlow, England • London • New York • Boston • San Francisco • Toronto • Sydney • Auckland • Singapore • Hong Kong
Tokyo • Seoul • Taipei • New Delhi • Cape Town • São Paulo • Mexico City • Madrid • Amsterdam • Munich • Paris • Milan

PEARSON EDUCATION LIMITED

Edinburgh Gate
Harlow CM20 2JE
Tel: +44 (0)1279 623623
Fax: +44 (0)1279 431059
Website: www.pearsoned.com/uk

First published in Great Britain in 2012

© Pearson Education Limited 2012

The right of Laurence French to be identified as author of this work has been asserted by him in accordance with the Copyright, Designs and Patents Act 1988.

Pearson Education is not responsible for the content of third party internet sites.

ISBN: 978-1-4082-8481-0

British Library Cataloguing-in-Publication Data
A catalogue record for this book is available from the British Library

Library of Congress Cataloging-in-Publication Data
French, Laurence.
    Brilliant supply teacher : what you need to know to be a truly outstanding teacher / Laurence French.
        p. cm.
    Includes bibliographical references and index.
    ISBN 978-1-4082-8481-0 (pbk.)
    1. Substitute teachers–Great Britain. 2. Effective teaching–Great Britain.
    I. Title.
    LB2844.1.S8F74 2012
    371.14'1220941–dc23
                        2011043054

10 9 8 7 6 5 4 3 2 1
15 14 13 12 11

Typeset in 10/14pt Plantin by 3
Printed and bound in Malaysia (CTP-VP)

I would like to dedicate this book to my late mother, who inspired me to become a teacher.

Contents

About the author

Laurence French has had over 35 years' experience as a teacher. Having graduated from the University of Warwick, Institute of Education, Laurence and his wife moved to Yorkshire where he taught in a middle school in Bradford. In 1977 they moved back to the Midlands where Laurence started working in secondary schools in Nuneaton and later in Leamington Spa.

Over the course of his career he was Head of English, Head of Faculty of Language and Communications, and twice Head of Sixth Form. He also worked for the University of Southampton Centre for Educational Marketing and lectured across the country on marketing and public relations for schools.

Laurence was a contributor to the *Schools' Management Handbook* between 1992 and 1995, writing about public relations and marketing for schools.

Laurence has written numerous articles over the years for educational magazines and journals and has made several radio and television appearances. In recent years he has worked as a supply teacher and as a one-to-one tutor.

Acknowledgements

I would like to thank the following people and institutions for all their help in researching material for this book: Brian Langley, Campion School, Leamington Spa; Ray Oram, supply teacher and good friend; Steve Long, supply teacher; Daljit Sandhu-Kooner, former supply teacher, now Head of Art, Campion School, Leamington Spa; Lynis Bassett, Class People Agency, Cheltenham; Lee Freeman, Monarch Recruitment Agency, Birmingham; Ruth Harris, Round Oak Special School, Warwick; Roy Evans, Kenilworth School, Kenilworth; Sue Davies, Deputy Head, Balsall Common Primary School; and finally, my wife, Angela for all her help and encouragement during the writing of this book.

Publisher's acknowledgements

We are grateful to the following for permission to reproduce copyright material:

Haydn's 10-point scale on pp.164–5, from 'How good is discipline in schools today?' by Terry Haydn, TES, www.tes.co.uk and quotes on p.191 from TES Connect forum, www.tes.co.uk/forums.

In some instances we have been unable to trace the owners of copyright material, and we would appreciate any information that would enable us to do so.

Preface

Entering the world of supply teaching is to some extent like taking a leap out of an aeroplane, hoping the parachute will open and that you will eventually land on your feet rather than be carted away in a body bag. This sounds somewhat dramatic, but the point is that sometimes you just never know what the day will bring when you work as a supply teacher.

It can be quite a daunting and intimidating venture in the early days, no matter what your level of experience as a teacher. A colleague of mine recently admitted to being terrified on her first day as a supply teacher, despite the fact that she was employed by the school in which she had been teaching for a number of years and was well known by all the students and staff.

As a supply teacher you will most likely be faced with the unfamiliar. You will probably find yourself in a school that you have never been to before. The students will be strangers to you ... and you to them, of course; subjects that you teach will not necessarily be your own specialisms; the staff you work with might or might not talk to you; you might or might not go back the next day, week or month. At the end of the day you might love the place and be happy to return (the 'happy landing on your feet' scenario) or alternatively you might never wish to set foot in the place again and barely escape in one piece, metaphorically speaking (the 'body bag' alternative). Either way, you'll probably have learnt more about yourself, the students and the vagaries of the British education system in one day than you've learnt in all your years as a teacher.

It can be quite an eye opener to walk into a large and sprawling inner city school of over 1000 students when you've been used to a cosy establishment of pleasant, co-operative, willing students in the leafy middle-class suburbs. Of course, the opposite also applies.

Not all inner city schools are educational war zones. Many are incredibly vibrant, exciting and innovative places which perform brilliantly given their often quite disadvantaged intake. Equally, not all leafy, suburban, middle-class schools with students from predominantly well-heeled aspirational families are a joy to work in either. The demands on staff, and therefore on you as a supply teacher, can be unrealistically high and can be difficult to cope with in long- and short-term appointments.

The general rule, therefore, is to be prepared for just about any eventuality, conditions and responses. After a while you will know which schools to avoid and which to grovel to your agency to return to. But just like preparing for your parachute jump, preparation, planning and experience are what count in the long run.

In this book I hope to cover as many aspects of the world of supply teaching as possible so that the aspiring applicant of whatever age and experience can feel confident in his or her role, and can have access to hints, tips and suggestions based on many years' experience to help make the job more enjoyable and fulfilling.

These will include:

- the supply teacher and agencies;
- emergency lesson planning;
- examples of good and bad practices;

- survival in the classroom;
- the life of a supply teacher;
- what sorts of people become supply teachers;
- using the internet for lesson ideas;
- the future of supply teaching.

There are several other books on the market devoted to the work of supply teaching. My advice is to read a few (starting with this one, of course) and find out about the job before embarking on it as a career choice or short-term expediency. Talk to other supply teachers and get the view from the 'chalkface'. There are a number of forums on the internet that can be helpful here. Try the 'TES Connect' one for a start.

If supply teaching is not for you, better to find out sooner rather than later. If it is for you, I wish you well in your career.

Laurence French

CHAPTER 1

What are supply teachers and who becomes one?

The simplest definition of a supply teacher is a qualified teacher who works on a temporary basis for whatever school requires their services for however long it needs them.

Qualifications

To become a supply teacher you need to have a recognised and validated teaching qualification from a UK or overseas educational institution, such as an Institute of Education of a university or teacher training establishment. These can be obtained by a variety of means such as:

- Post-Graduate Certificate of Education (PGCE) courses;
- School-Centred Initial Teacher Training (SCITT) or Graduate Teacher Programme (GTP);
- overseas candidates from outside the EU will need to go through the Overseas Trained Teacher Programme before being deemed qualified to teach in a UK school.

Whatever route you take, you will need to gain Qualified Teacher Status (QTS) before you can apply for a post as a supply teacher. This is gained when you have completed your academic course, PGCE and newly qualified teacher (NQT) year.

The 16-month rule

If you are an NQT contemplating supply work, you need to be aware of the 16-month rule. From the first day of short-term supply, NQTs can continue supply work for 16 consecutive calendar months. This is regardless of whether the NQT undertakes that work for just one half-day or every weekday during the year.

For example, if an NQT starts short-term supply on 1 January 2011, their entitlement to short-term supply ends on 30 April 2012, regardless of how many days they have worked, or whether they did inductable work in between. Once this 16 months has passed, NQTs working in maintained schools or non-maintained special schools should cease short-term supply work unless they are granted an extension to the 16-month supply rule.

The role of the supply teacher

A supply teacher is not a full-time, permanent member of staff and, as such, their position in school is not that of a full-time, mainstream subject specialist or general teacher, but more of a temporary, flexible, adaptable general teacher who is expected to be able to handle any age group and any subject within the school. This could mean that you find yourself teaching Year 7 maths through to Year 11 GCSE PE and all subjects in between. You could be in front of a top group of highly motivated, aspirational Year 11 biology students, all of whom are intending to go on to be top surgeons, or a bottom set Year 7 group whose attainment varies from Level 2 to Level 4 with very poor standards of literacy and numeracy. You might be in front of a small group of Year 3 pupils doing interesting and creative art work or 35 Year 6 pupils teaching numeracy. You could even find yourself teaching reception classes in a primary school. As a supply teacher you will be expected to cope with both extremes. On occasions you might find yourself in a special school. I will discuss the differences between the various phases (primary and secondary) and special schools in Chapter 4 later.

You are not employed by the school and your source of income will vary from that of a full-time, mainstream teacher. However, you will be paid according to your position on the pay scales if you work for a local authority pool, and some agencies will also negotiate the same pay deal for you. Your rights and responsibilities will probably be different depending on the school you work for; your workload will be different and your status within the school will be different. Despite these factors, you are a teacher and are expected to teach, not babysit. All these points will be covered in more depth throughout the book.

There are a number of other allied classroom positions with which you might find yourself working or in competition. I have included a brief review of these below as newcomers to the profession might not necessarily be aware of them and what their role is. Equally, for some unqualified aspiring teachers, these routes might be a valuable way of gaining experience before becoming fully qualified or starting a PGCE year.

Teaching assistants

A teaching assistant (TA) is different from a supply teacher. They will usually be unqualified classroom helpers responsible for an individual student who has special educational needs of some sort, or who is acting as a general classroom helper under the direction of the teacher. TAs often help the mainstream teachers with such tasks as small group work or creating displays for the classroom. They are not normally left in charge of a class without supervision.

Cover supervisors

A cover supervisor – a relatively new post in schools – is *usually* an unqualified staff member whose job it is to supervise classes for a limited period in the absence of their regular teacher. Cover supervisors are not expected to teach the classes they supervise, although in my experience many of them do simply because standing in front of a class supervising can be deadly boring and in many cases undesirable from a disciplinary and educational point of view. A note of caution: many schools are now employing cover supervisors in place of supply teachers as they are permanent staff members and a lot cheaper to employ.

One-to-one tutors

This is another relatively new area in schools in which qualified or unqualified staff act as one-to-one tutors for a selected group of pupils. These might comprise, for example, Looked After Children or those with particular problems in numeracy or literacy development. Some of these tutors will be using this experience to enhance their chances of gaining their QTS at a later stage.

A supply teacher's life is varied, unpredictable and often seasonal in nature and one can sometimes feel a bit like the 'hired gun' beloved of Western movies. You go in, do the job and move on, sometimes unnoticed or unappreciated. However, for the short time you are there, you will have left your mark in one way or another.

Who becomes a supply teacher, and why?

Supply teaching is not for everyone. Before deciding on taking that career route you would do well to think it through carefully and make your decision based on real knowledge of the job, not just on a vague notion of 'how nice it will be not to have to work if I don't want to' or 'thank goodness I won't have to spend my time writing pointless reports and attending tedious meetings'. Truth is, you might have to do those things as a supply teacher as well.

I hope that within the pages of this book you will find enough information and advice to enable you to make the right decision regarding working as a supply teacher.

I suspect that there are a significant number of people who choose supply teaching for the freedom and flexibility it affords, and who might well have spent many years in the classroom and for a variety of reasons need to have time for other aspects of their lives, such as bringing up children or looking after elderly relatives. It allows you to work part-time more easily than trying to negotiate a part-time contract with your school. Headteachers prefer not to encourage part-time work because of the time-tabling constraints it imposes and the lack of continuity it creates within the various subject areas.

Women returning to teaching after having children often find supply work particularly attractive because of its flexibility and the fact that, to a much greater degree than any other members of the profession, you can decide when or if you want to work. The obvious downside to this is, of course, that you have a somewhat unpredictable income stream, but as long as you are not the main breadwinner of the family or you are prepared for the uncertainties of your earning capacity, supply work can give you valuable additional income and still leave you time to 'have a life'.

Retired teachers who just can't drag themselves away from their beloved profession are another source of supply staff. Some do it to supplement their pension, though it should be said that for teachers who have retired recently their teachers' pensions are usually quite generous provided they have put in all the required years. That will come to an end as the profession moves to 'average salary' pensions, as opposed to 'final salary' pensions and I believe we'll see more retired teachers opting to do supply work in future.

I think, more importantly, many retirees opt for supply work to 'keep their hand in', so to speak. It's a good way of getting out of the house, keeping the brain active, mixing with other people, albeit those you don't know very well, if at all! One often overlooked benefit of retirees taking on supply work is that they might well bring with them years of experience as classroom practitioners and subject specialists. Most will have seen just about everything that schools can throw at them; some will be former senior teachers, heads of departments, pastoral heads and so on. That wealth of experience can and should be highly valued by schools when looking for supply staff.

These assertions are borne out by a 2010 survey conducted by the NASUWT that found that some 41% of respondents stated that they worked as supply staff as a means of supplementing their pensions; 11% said that they did the job because they were unable to secure a full-time post in teaching. Included in this figure are those who are aged under 35 years, those who have some form of disability and those who come from black or minority ethnic backgrounds. Of the others, 31% replied that they chose it as a deliberate career choice.

In November 2010, according to the BBC, graduate unemployment was running at 9%. The national unemployment rate at the same time was 7.7%. Approximately 21,000 graduate students were unemployed. Some of those would have been graduates completing their teacher training. This pool of incipient teaching talent needed to find jobs. They could, presumably, have found work in some low-paid, menial capacity or just sat at home watching day-time television and claiming unemployment benefits. Some would have applied for TA posts or cover supervisors. Many will have found employment as supply teachers: it is a way of getting your foot on the ladder, gaining experience for, hopefully, later full-time employment as a teacher. I should flag up a note of caution if you are newly qualified and thinking of supply work. From a school's point of view, recent graduates are often not the best prospects to put in front of a class. Their youthfulness is not always a benefit and I have seen such people becoming too friendly with students and even going out and socialising with some of the older ones in secondary schools.

Recent graduates are untested in the classroom, other than having completed their teaching practices. Their subject knowledge has not been refined and well-honed and they often make some appalling mistakes in their lessons. However, it is a starting point when fewer and fewer full-time posts are available.

On the plus side, they can bring new ideas to schools and energise departments with their enthusiasm and vitality. They are more willing than some to take on tasks which, strictly speaking, they should not be asked to do, but in order to gain experience willingly do so. And of course, if they are any good, they might just find themselves a job at a school they have worked in as a supply teacher. I have personal experience of some who have done exactly that, one of whom is now a head of department.

Newly qualified teachers going into supply work should maximise the opportunities to network and build contacts with the schools they work in. These can be invaluable later on, especially if a full-time post is advertised. It's a great way of proving yourself and getting known by the people who matter. It also provides evidence for your CV so you don't have to explain that embarrassing gap in your employment record. As a newly qualified teacher, you should join a teaching union as well. You'd be surprised at how many NQTs are unaware of the role and benefits of unions in their careers, particularly the legal representation and protection they afford.

As graduate unemployment increases and fewer full-time posts become available, supply teaching might be the only route graduates have to get into the profession.

Teaching has become one of the most stressful jobs over the past 20 or so years. Constant changes to curricula, the demanding and frightening inspection regime, targets, assessments, lesson observations, changes to working conditions, pay freezes and cuts all add to the pressure on the classroom teacher as well as on senior leaders and middle managers (HoDs, pastoral heads, etc.). For some, the pressure is too much and it has taken the fun out of teaching, removing the very reasons they went into the job in the first place.

I became an English teacher in the mid-1970s and loved the creative freedom it gave me, untrammelled by the myriad constraints imposed by exam boards and a succession of Secretaries of State for Education who insisted on leaving their stamp on the nation's schools. Practically all of that freedom has now disappeared and English teaching 'ain't what it used to be'.

As a result of these changes, some teachers have had enough of the full-time daily slog, have become demoralised and demotivated and have turned to supply work instead. I've heard many teachers say, with total honesty and frankness, that they can't wait to retire, and that another 20 years or whatever in the classroom is just too much to contemplate. It is a sad reflection on what has happened to education and to teachers in the UK that far too many think that way. Freedom, flexibility, the reduction of responsibilities and duties that come with supply teaching are very appealing to people like that and for them supply work can be their life-line. And until quite recently, there has been sufficient work to be had as a supply teacher. For the experienced person, the pay is not bad either.

The assumption I have made about the people who want to

become supply teachers is that they are UK citizens, with degrees and teaching qualifications gained here. What of overseas teachers who want to work in the UK as supply teachers? Some will want to do it as a full-time or part-time job; others as a stepping stone to full-time regular employment as a teacher. How do they fare in the supply market?

Overseas applicants fall roughly into two camps – those from within the EU and those from other parts of the world.

Briefly, teachers in the UK and from the EU are automatically granted QTS providing they have gained:

- a Bachelor of Education (B.Ed.) degree,
- a Post-Graduate Certificate of Education, or
- passed a Graduate Teacher Programme.

They must also have completed an induction year (NQT).

Teachers from the EU should also contact the General Teaching Council to ensure their qualifications are equivalent to UK qualifications.

If the candidate is from Australia, New Zealand, South Africa or Canada they will not have QTS, but most UK schools will recognise that their teaching qualification is suitable for them to teach in a UK school.

Teachers who trained outside the European Economic Area (EEA) and who are not nationals of an EEA country can work for up to four years in Britain as a temporary, unqualified teacher without the need for QTS. However, to gain full teacher qualifications they would have to go through the Overseas Trained Teacher Programme (OTTP) that lasts a year. For them supply work could provide valuable experience if they are intending to stay in the UK and make a career out of teaching. This is, of course, contingent on the candidate having the correct work permits and visas allowing them to work in the UK.

Working as an unqualified supply teacher will, of course, affect your earning capacity. It is roughly half of a qualified teacher's income, with the latest approximate figures from the TDA for 2011 at £16,000–£26,000 p.a. (London rates) and £15,000–£25,000 p.a. outside London.

Non-EU applicants, including those from the Commonwealth, wanting to work as supply teachers will have to obtain a National Recognition Information Centre for the United Kingdom (NARIC) assessment form to prove that their qualifications are equivalent to UK qualifications.

According to the NARIC website, you will need to submit the following documents:

- a photocopy of your certificates together with final transcripts;
- a covering letter with your contact details stating the purpose of your enquiry;
- a photocopy of a certified translation in English (if necessary);
- a self-addressed envelope with correct postage if the letter is for a UK address (if the postal address is outside the UK, you do not need to provide postage);
- a pre-paid special delivery envelope if a recorded mail service is required for the delivery of your letter and return of documents to a UK address: if the return of documents is required to an address outside the UK, it is your responsibility to arrange an appropriate courier service.

Full details can be found at **www.naric.org.uk**.

If you are an overseas applicant for supply work and English is not your first language, it is not unreasonable that schools will expect that you have a good command of written and spoken English; that you are familiar with current National Curriculum requirements; that you understand how to plan and deliver lessons in an environment which might be very different from the one you have come from, and that you have some understanding of the culture in which you are working and living. I have personal experience of how the lack of those attributes and skills can adversely affect a supply teacher's chances of employment.

The following case studies are all based on my personal experience and highlight the importance of being fully qualified and conversant with the UK education system before embarking on either supply work or full-time permanent teaching posts. Improbable though they might appear, I can assure you they are all genuine.

I have also included them to show how situations can get out of hand and as an object lesson on how to behave – or not – in schools when on a supply contract.

🡕 brilliant case studies

Background

Some years ago I was head of the Language and Communications Faculty at my secondary school. I had a staff of 13 full- and part-time teachers across 4 departments. It was a demanding, but very fulfilling job. One Wednesday, a long-serving colleague informed me that he was taking medical leave to have a hip replacement operation. Naturally I thought he meant it would be in a week or two or during the summer holiday which was a term away; however, by the following Monday he was gone. That left the English department with a major problem. He had a full timetable, including two GCSE classes, that we had to cover.

Before the days of 'Rarely Cover' – a system recently introduced which limits the amount of cover teachers are expected to do – internal staff covered staff absence, and this is what happened to start with, but it was obvious it couldn't go on for long. I spent much of the first few days planning lessons for my colleague's classes.

We needed someone who could take on a long-term contract of at least three-quarters of a term, until we could find a permanent replacement or my colleague returned. We contacted an agency that we had used before and they sent us a supply teacher.

Teacher #1

He arrived about a week after my colleague had left. He had worked for us before and as far as we knew was trustworthy. As his classroom was opposite mine, I could keep an eye on things until I was satisfied that he had settled in and was coping well. For the first week or so he seemed to be fine. I had had no complaints from staff or students and from my observations he was doing a reasonable job. I was happy.

Then the problems arose. First, a junior colleague came to me and said that Teacher #1 had told her that he knew where she lived and had offered to give her a lift to and from school each day. She said she'd never seen him before and had never told him where she lived or anything about herself. She was, naturally, very wary and wanted to alert me to the situation, which had made her feel uncomfortable. I asked her to let me know if it happened again. Maybe it was innocent and he was just being nice. Maybe it was more sinister.

Some days later she came to me again and complained. He'd obviously been making a nuisance of himself and she was now genuinely worried. I took Teacher #1 to one side and explained the situation and asked him not to approach her again. He gave me an assurance that he would not mention it to her again. As far as I was concerned the matter was over and my junior colleague was satisfied with the outcome.

The next thing that happened was that a member of the office staff told me that Teacher #1 had spent several of his free periods in the medical room, which was situated next to the main office, on the phone – the school one – to his lawyer. When I tackled him about this he admitted that he was currently embroiled in a court case and needed to speak to his solicitor regularly. Not on our time, I told him. And he hadn't paid for the calls either!

By now I was beginning to think that things couldn't get much worse and that we might have to take more formal proceedings against him, such as an interview with the head and his union rep. Before that could happen, however, things did get worse.

One day a very upset student knocked on my classroom door mid-lesson and asked to see me urgently. She reported that Teacher #1 had just told one of our overseas students that she should go back to her own country. The student in question was very upset and was in tears in the corridor outside my room.

When I asked Teacher #1 about this he admitted it. Within 10 minutes he and I were in the head's office and I told the head about all the problems we'd encountered with him. Within 30 minutes Teacher #1 was escorted off the premises, his agency was informed and he never worked as a supply teacher again.

Back to square one! We contacted the agency again and asked if they had anyone else who could take on the rest of the period to the end of term. They sent us another supply teacher.

Teacher #2

He was middle aged, very well spoken and was an English specialist. Just what we needed ... until I found out that his only experience teaching English was in an ex-pat. private school in Saudi Arabia teaching groups of six or seven well-heeled young men from the English community out there. He had never taught in England, had little or no knowledge of UK education, the National Curriculum, marking and assessment criteria or how to deliver a lesson to a full class of students.

We persevered with him for a week, but it was very clear he wasn't going to make it. I sat in on a number of lessons and my heart sank every time. Had I not been there, I think his classes would have probably rioted just out of frustration at his ineptitude.

He left at the end of his first week.

Back to the agency ...

▶

Teacher #3

He was young, African and barely spoke English. He'd only recently arrived in England, had no knowledge of UK education, the National Curriculum, and so on. The students could hardly understand a word he said, and though he tried desperately to do the job to our satisfaction, it was not going to work. I gave him master classes on lesson preparation, delivery, marking and assessment procedures, how to handle a scheme of work, where all our resources were and what was available to him. Little of it made any difference and he left after a week.

Back to the agency ...

Teacher #4

We were now in the final half term of the year when she arrived. She was young, attractive, confident, vivacious and very clever. My confidence in supply teachers had now been totally sapped and despite all her positive qualities, I was sceptical and held out little hope of her staying beyond the week.

On her first morning, I had a free period, so I did what I normally did and that was to do my 'management by walking about' routine, dipping in and out of classes to see what was happening, talking to staff and students about their work. As I was going down a corridor, I beheld a sight that gladdened my heart. At the beginning of the lesson, she had her class lined up like little soldiers outside the classroom ready to go in. She was standing in front of them marshalling them, with a smile and a greeting, into the room in silence.

I came back later in the lesson and stood, unseen, outside her door. It was obvious that she had them eating out of the palm of her hand. At break time the same day she asked if it would be all right if she wrote a scheme of work for one of the classes that was different from the ones we had in the department. I gladly gave her the go-ahead.

The students loved her; she was very popular in the staffroom, fitting in with the rest of the departmental staff as if she'd known them all her life; brought in cakes at lunchtime for the department and generally behaved as if she were a regular member of staff. Books were marked every day, lessons were planned competently and delivered with enthusiasm. I never once had to intervene in a lesson to sort out any problem. I couldn't believe my luck.

She stayed with us for the rest of the term and was offered the full-time post now vacated by my sick colleague who had decided to take early retirement. But as the Bible says: 'The Lord giveth and the Lord taketh away.' She had decided not to stay in teaching and had applied to join the RAF Intelligence Unit, for which she had been accepted and was due to start later that year. No amount of persuasion, sweet talking or grovelling could change her mind. She was a great loss to our school and profession and I'm sure if she'd stayed she would have developed into an outstanding teacher. However, she had her own plans and, as far as I know, she has carved out a successful career in the armed forces.

I would hope my experiences here are not typical, but whether you are a supply teacher reading this or a school cover manager, I think there are valuable lessons to be learnt.

If you are intending to go into supply work, make sure you are properly equipped and qualified, that your knowledge and skills are up-to-date and that you are familiar with the expectations that schools have of their supply staff. A thorough knowledge of the broad aims and objectives of the National Curriculum are invaluable, even if you do not have specific subject knowledge. You need to know how to plan and deliver successful, inspiring lessons as you cannot always rely on schools providing you with work, especially if you are on a long-term supply assignment.

If you are working in a school and one of your responsibilities is to book and look after supply staff, don't just take the word of the agency about their competency in the classroom. Although there are myriad checks made on supply staff before being assigned to schools, including usually two professional references, competency in the classroom is not one of them. Only you can judge that by observation in the classroom. If you have any doubts about the competency of your supply staff, it is important to tackle it as soon as possible with the supply teacher and, if necessary, with their agency.

Making a career out of supply teaching

I have been asked if it is possible to make a career from being a supply teacher. I suppose the honest answer to that question is based on how you define 'career'.

A career implies a progression through one's chosen profession, with regular training and updating of current requirements, trends and advances and so on, along with increased responsibilities and duties. It suggests that there is a definite path open to you and that you will progress along it over the course of your working life. Can you do this with supply work?

I think the simple answer is no. You can, however, make a very decent living from it and, if you are lucky and well prepared, you might find that you can work five days a week on a fairly regular basis. It depends, of course, on your personal circumstances and skills as well as the geographical area you live in.

In order to develop your skills, you might be invited to take part in a school's continuing professional development (CPD) programme if you are on a long-term assignment, or join your department's training sessions. These will help update your skills and knowledge and could be valuable additional material for your CV later on. As a supply teacher, you cannot rely on this happening. Schools do not always view their supply staff in the same way as they do their regular staff.

Unlike the opportunities given to a full-time teacher, these courses will not necessarily aid your progression through your work as a supply teacher. The job is too transitory and unpredictable for that to happen. To be sure of true career development, you need to be working as a full-time regular member of a school staff.

What makes a good supply teacher?

The sorts of qualities that make a good supply teacher are, of course, broadly the same as those for any teacher. However, supply teachers are different in many ways and to be a good supply teacher it's important to bear in mind the following points:

- Flexibility – supply teachers need to be flexible in terms of what assignments to take on and what they have to teach when they get to an assignment. You might spend most of your time out of your subject 'comfort zone'.

- Plan ahead – do not assume that work will be ready waiting for you when you arrive at the school. Always have a store of starter activities, lessons or interactive ideas that can be done in an IT suite.

- Plan your journey – as Woody Allen famously said '90% of success is showing up'. Unless you have to travel a long distance at very short notice, make sure you arrive at your school in good time.

- Resources – bring your own. Have a stock of such mundane things as pencils, pens, rulers, an A4 pad, a mug, a packed lunch. You won't know until you get there what is or is not available.

- Make yourself known to staff and pupils.

- Take an interest in the life of the school, especially if you are going to be there for a long time.

- Ask about routines, timetables and procedures for disciplining and rewarding children. Remember, pupils do not generally like a change to their routine. If you can slot into their daily work pattern as soon as possible, you will find life a lot easier.

- Familiarise yourself with the management structure. Find out whom to see about what.

- Get to know your groups as soon as possible. Remember, they will still be there after you have left. Don't treat them as aliens!

- Stay calm and confident. After all, if you don't like the school, you don't have to go back.

Registering as a supply teacher

Provided you are registered as a teacher with the General Teaching Council, you could look on the Schools Recruitment Service website for vacancies (**www.schoolsrecruitment.dcsf. gov.uk**) or contact your local authority (LA) to see if it operates a supply pool. Some do; others have outsourced this to private companies such as Eteach (**www.eteach.com**).

Alternatively, approach an agency. The *Times Educational Supplement* (TES) carries advertisements for agencies, as does the web, of course. Most agencies have an on-line registration form, and after filling that in you will most likely be called in for an interview.

You could also approach a school directly, but it would be unwise to do it this way if the school does not know you as it will be faced with conducting its own checks before employing you. It is more likely to go through its LA supply pool or an agency if it wants supply teachers where the multitude of checks will have already been completed. I will discuss the checking procedures in full in Chapter 2.

Questions to ask yourself

1 Why do I want to become a supply teacher instead of a full-time teacher?

2 Am I prepared for the uncertainties of working as a supply teacher?

3 Do I fit the criteria of what makes a good supply teacher?

4 Do I mind getting up early or receiving early morning calls from agencies or schools?

5 Can I cope with the travelling that comes with being a supply teacher?

6 Have I really got what it takes?

 brilliant recap

- If you are planning on becoming a supply teacher, check you have the appropriate qualifications for teaching, GTC and union membership.

- Think about why you want to become a supply teacher. It's not for everyone and it can be very demanding.

- Becoming a cover supervisor or teaching assistant is a possible way in to supply teaching as this will give you valuable classroom experience before gaining QTS.

- You won't make a career out of supply teaching, but you can make a decent living.

- Make sure you fully understand what makes a good supply teacher and what your role is.

CHAPTER 2

Finding work and getting started

Make no mistake about it, supply teaching is big business. The General Teaching Council (GTC) estimates that there are approximately 50,000 supply teachers in England and Wales at any one time. That is about 9% of the total teaching force. Now, just for sake of argument, let's say that all of those teachers are working on one particular day. Let's also say, just for the sake of argument, that they all earn £120 a day. That makes a total of £6 million in daily earnings. If only half of those available are working, that's still a huge amount of money changing hands on a daily basis.

Little wonder, then, that recruitment agencies are doing good business and have proliferated over the past few years. In fact, they are now the main recruiters of supply teachers in this country, whereas not too long ago the local authority (LA) supply pool was the main source. With the cutbacks in public spending in 2010, and the consequent effects that will have on local authorities, along with changes to their role regarding education, LAs are even less likely to be involved in the supply teacher pool. Many have already outsourced this function to private companies.

However, at the moment it is still possible to find work in other ways without going to an agency.

Direct approach to schools

One way is to approach a school directly, but unless you are known to them, perhaps as a former teacher or someone connected with the school on a voluntary basis, you might find that you are limited in how much work is available. Cover managers (usually, but not exclusively, deputy heads) will have numerous speculative letters from aspiring supply teachers and will need to trawl through these in order to find 'the suitable person' on the day. Frankly, I have yet to meet a deputy head who has the time or inclination to do this at 8 a.m. when someone has just rung in sick. Unless you are a regular at the school and a trusted supply teacher, your chances of regular work might be somewhat diminished. However, don't dismiss this option. In the NASUWT survey 'Current Working Conditions and Experiences of Supply Teachers' (2008) 53% of the respondents stated that they found work through direct approaches to and personal contact with schools so it is worth pursuing if you have good contacts and a sound reputation with the schools in question.

Even if you are successful in attracting the attention of the cover manager, a school will – or should – insist on a number of checks being carried out before employing you. I do know that some schools have developed their own checking system, but it is by no means a common practice and will probably not be as rigorous as that of an agency. It is also very time consuming for the school. At the very least you will need Criminal Record Bureau (CRB) documentation.

Personal recommendation from a member of staff might secure you a supply teacher position, but as stated above you might find it reduces your scope. For one thing, you are limiting your opportunities for work as other schools in your area will not necessarily know you and therefore not feel obliged to employ you if the work dries up. What work you do get will also be sporadic and limited in scope if you are working for one particular school all the time. In any case most schools have contact with one or more agencies these days and will most likely stick to that arrangement. As you will see below, it's much easier that way for the school.

Local authority supply pools

Local authority supply pools are the next source of work for the supply teacher. Contacting your local authority through its website might elicit the result you are after, but while researching for this book, I looked at a number of county and city council sites and not one of them had any useful information about, or vacancies for, supply teachers. This probably indicates that the majority of local authorities have now outsourced this facility to agencies or have combined with other authorities to form their own agency. Eteach currently operates the supply pool for over a third of the local authorities in England and Wales. In the same NASUWT survey only 13% of teachers stated that they were employed through local authority pools and only 8% said they obtain ad hoc supply work through their local authority pool on a day-to-day basis.

However, it is still a viable option and has some distinct advantages. If you have worked for the LA previously it will have your details on file already and you will be a known quantity in terms of your employment record, length of service and general reputation as a teacher. The other main advantage is that the rates of pay from a local authority supply pool are more advantageous to you than those from an agency. This is because local authorities pay you according to your position on the national pay scales for teachers, whereas agencies can set their own rates of pay.

Rates of pay for supply teachers working for a LA or directly with schools

Your pay is calculated on the basis of 1/195 of the appropriate pay scale, that being the number of teaching days in an academic year for a full-time teacher. Under the School Teachers' Review Body (STRB) regulations it includes an element for 'holiday pay' as well, even though you do not receive holiday pay per se in the same way as a full-time teacher.

You will be paid usually on a daily rate, but it is possible also that you might be paid an hourly figure if, for example, you only worked two hours (maybe two periods for an afternoon) or just an odd period here and there.

One major teaching union, the NUT, has recommended that that the daily rate should be 1/950 of the annual salary, whereas the Department for Education calculates it on the basis of 1/195 of the annual salary divided by 6.48, the number of working hours in a day.

For example, let's say your full-time salary was £35,000. Your hourly rate according to the NUT recommendation would be 1/950 of £35,000 = £36.84 per hour. The DfE rate, though, would only give you 1/195 of £35,000 divided by 6.48 = £27.70 per hour, a considerable difference especially if you are not making a full-time occupation out of supply work.

Daily rates

In terms of daily rates, that will depend to some extent on the geographical area in which you are teaching. Wherever you work, though, you will be paid according to your position on the national pay scales, with qualifications and experience taken into account.

Taking the same base level as an example (Main Pay Scale point 6) you can see from the figures opposite the differences you can expect depending on where you teach:

Inner London
Annual Salary: £36,387
Daily Rate: £186.60

Outer London
Annual Salary: £35,116
Daily Rate: £180.08

Fringe Area
Annual Salary: £32,588
Daily Rate: £167.12

Rest of E & W
Annual Salary: £31,552
Daily Rate: £161.81

brilliant tip

All teachers employed by a local authority are also entitled to an incremental progression on the pay spine each year. You should receive an additional spine point for experience in September each year, *provided you have worked for at least 26 weeks in the previous 12 months*, until you reach the top of the main pay scale. You are also entitled to go through the threshold onto the upper pay scale while working as a supply teacher.

It is very important, therefore, to keep a log of the hours/days you have worked throughout the year, and how much you have earned in that time.

Signing with an agency

Signing up with an agency is a popular and usually successful way to get work as a supply teacher. The survey from the NASUWT stated that 40% of applicants under 35 years of age are likely to be employed through an agency. In recent years they have increased in number and just a quick search on the internet will show how many there are to choose from. The question is, how do you know if you've chosen the right one?

Agencies vary in size and location, as well as in their 'specialism'. Some specialise in all phases of education from nursery schools to secondary schools and into higher education; others specialise in just the primary phase or the secondary phase. A quick phone call or internet search will tell you what you need to know.

Before looking at agencies in more depth, just a word about rates of pay – always a topic that the incipient supply teacher is interested in.

Agencies are not bound by the same regulations regarding pay for supply teachers, as those working for a local authority or directly with a school, i.e. the School Teachers' Pay and Conditions Document (STPCD).

Instead, supply teachers working for an agency are subject to pay and conditions *determined by the individual agency*. In addition, periods of employment from an agency are not pensionable under the Teachers' Pension Scheme. Consequently, many agencies undercut the national pay rates and conditions of service that would apply to supply teachers working for a local authority or individual school.

To give you some example of how agency rates of pay can vary, these advertised rates appeared in November 2010 in a local newspaper. They were from several agencies, national and local:

- **Year 5 teacher needed for a term**: £105–£145 per day
- **Science teacher:** £103–£140 per day
- **Science teacher** (expected to take on the role of a class teacher): £100–£149 per day
- **English teacher**: competitive rates (sic).

Working for an agency will mean that you are responsible for getting your weekly timesheet to them on time, making sure first that the school has authorised it.

tip

Tax and National Insurance are deducted by the agency; if you work for more than one agency it is a good idea to nominate one of them as your main source of income for tax purposes. Keep your local tax office up-to-date with what you are doing.

tip

Always check pay rates with any agency you approach before signing with them.

Ironically, most supply teachers like to work for an agency despite the caveats mentioned above. The reasons are fairly obvious. Agencies can get you far more work than your LA; though the rates of pay are generally lower, the work is more frequent and provided you are prepared to travel and do not mind what assignments you are sent on, you can most likely work as many days as you want. Most supply teachers I have met are with more than one agency and so can pick and choose what jobs to accept and where to work.

A good agency will hold training courses for its supply teachers. One small, independent agency in Cheltenham regularly holds seminars in a local hotel on continuing professional development (CPD), handling discipline problems in schools and instructions in the 'tricks of the trade', particularly for newcomers.

A large national agency I spoke to holds training courses for their cover supervisors and teaching assistants as well as for their supply teachers. The delegates are sometimes asked to pay a contribution to these courses.

Yet another large agency told me that 'all teachers have access to [their] extensive CPD programme'. They also have 'a range of face-to-face courses, distance learning programmes and teacher forums ... provided free of charge'.

As long as agencies do what they say they do, then supply teachers have a valuable and fairly comprehensive back-up system to rely on to ensure that, as far as possible, they can progress through their 'career' in supply work and feel confident that should anything go wrong, they have support.

The advantages to the supply teacher of signing with an agency are:

- There is usually a reliable frequency of work.
- With large agencies, a consultant will be there to support and guide you.
- The agency will handle any problems you might have with a school.
- Most large and medium-size agencies will monitor your work and will liaise with the schools on its books.
- Larger agencies will hold training courses for their supply teachers.

From a school's point of view, securing a supply teacher through an agency is preferable as long as the agency is reputable. Some concerns have been expressed about the quality of some supply teachers from agencies who might well be putting teachers into positions for which they are not suited or qualified for the sake of profit to the agency. Agencies that do this should be avoided. Also, of course, the school has to pay the agency for its services. However, a reputable agency will work with schools to ensure the 'right person' is placed in the schools and that the school is happy with the financial arrangements it has with the agency. Most big agencies negotiate with individual schools and teachers to ensure the right financial package is in place.

The benefits, therefore, for the school are:

- A single call to an agency hands over the problem to them and takes the pressure off the hard-pressed deputy or cover manager.

- Agencies have a large number of supply teachers to call on and will be far more successful in placing the right person to the right school.

- Agency checks will have been conducted in a thorough way (more on those later!) and the supply teacher will be known to the agency and will most likely have worked for it previously.

A good agency works on the basis of trust with its schools and as long as it can keep supplying teachers who are competent class-room practitioners, who do a good job for the school and thus for the agency, schools will keep coming back to that agency for their supply teachers. It becomes, therefore, mutually beneficial and a long-term relationship can be built up between the school and the agency it works with. This will, in the end, pay enormous dividends for all parties concerned.

This arrangement takes a lot of the pressure off schools and makes the job of finding a supply teacher much easier, espe-cially on those occasions when several teachers ring in sick on a Monday morning or when the dreaded winter flu bug does its dastardly work in the staffroom. At times like that, you need a fast track, reliable and fool-proof system if you are the one in charge of booking supply teachers. And you can always blame the agency if it doesn't work out!

Contacting an agency

Choose your agency carefully. Decide what phases of educa-tion you want to work in, what type of supply work you are interested in and find an agency that specialises in that phase or has a national reputation that you can rely on. Avoid what one agency called 'the high street outfit', those who are not nationally accredited, whose sole function appears to be the random placement of teachers in schools for maximum profit for themselves. This could result in your being sent to a school placement that is entirely unsuited to you or one to which you have no prior experience or expertise, such as a special school. Anyone can set up as an agency, but not everyone can make a success of it!

The Quality Mark

brilliant tip

Look for an agency with the Quality Mark, issued by the Department for Education.

The Quality Mark was launched in 2002 as a joint initiative between the Department for Children, Schools and Families and the Recruitment and Employment Confederation (REC) to help drive up standards.

It sets minimum standards for agencies to reach in the ways they recruit and interview supply teachers, the way they monitor performance and the way they keep abreast of all changes that occur in teaching. All good recruitment agencies should hold a Quality Mark accreditation which will be displayed on its brochures and website. While not an absolute guarantee of competence or quality, it is a good indicator of the sorts of services you can expect from it.

Application to an agency

Assuming you contact an agency through the internet, you will find an on-line application form to fill in. Once you have sent that off, the agency will then get to work on your application.

In a big agency, a recruitment consultant will normally be assigned to you and will work with you throughout your time with it. Be aware though, that like any other field of employment, there is always a turnover of staff. If you are lucky you'll have a consultant who will be staying for some time with the agency. However, supply teachers have told me that in some cases, they have ended up chasing the work themselves because of a lack of continuity with their agency consultant.

While you are with the agency, you will be able to build up a strong working relationship with your consultant and you will find therefore that the work that is offered to you is suited to your talents, expertise, preferences and qualifications as far as possible.

The normal procedure will then be for the agency to call you in for a face-to-face, in-depth interview. At this point you will need to take with you a bundle of documents. The number of these will depend on the agency, but all good agencies will require basic information from you and you will not be able to work without certain checks being made beforehand.

A large national agency that I talked to required more documents than a smaller, independent agency. However, both agencies were adamant about the rigour of their selection process and the checks they carried out, and both agencies carried the Quality Mark.

To give you some idea of what is required, the following is a list from a large, well-respected national agency:

- passport or visa if required;
- driving licence or other form of photo ID;
- birth certificate (if passport cannot be provided);
- National Insurance card/payslip;
- two address proofs (from past three months);
- proof of qualifications (or Naric details);

- proof of GTC registration;
- evidence of any name changes;
- five-year address history;
- current enhanced CRB;
- two professional references;
- medical details.

While most of these will be relatively easy to locate, you do need to be aware that some can take quite a long time to come through. References, for example, can take time if the referee forgets or regards it as a low priority item on their 'must do' list.

CRB documents can also take an age – four to six weeks seems to be the average time to get one through. This will be even longer if you have moved house several times as the CRB documentation gives a five-year history of where you have lived. If you have moved house often, the checks have to be made at every police station in each area. If you are from abroad, the checks have to be made to the relevant overseas authorities which could add months to your application time. However, without your CRB documentation, you will not secure a position as a supply teacher.

The cost of a CRB check is £44.00 (2011 figure) but some agencies will refund you this after you have worked for them for a while.

You will also be checked to ensure that you are not on List 99, the national database of sex offenders. It goes without saying that if you are on that list you will never secure a position in teaching.

At the face-to-face interview with an agency consultant your documentation will be thoroughly checked and you will be assessed as to your suitability to work as a supply teacher. During the interview your spoken and written English might be assessed as well and any recommendations about your competency – or lack of – will be offered if the agency feels that you are not up to par.

As with any interview, your personal demeanour and appearance, attitudes, friendliness, willingness to be flexible in your approach and determination to succeed are all being judged. The agency also has to be sure that you are going to be a 'saleable asset' and that you will do nothing to damage the reputation of the agency when you are on a teaching assignment. I have seen and heard many comments by supply teachers over the years denigrating their agencies for a variety of perceived misdemeanours. Whether they are justified or not is beside the point, but in these days of publicly accessed web-based communications, it is unwise to publicise your grievances on-line if you want to continue to work for them. A good agency has to be sure it has a professional and responsible teacher on its books and one on whom it can rely for complete integrity.

brilliant timesaver

If you are expecting simply to sign on with an agency and start work the next week, forget it! You will need to factor in a sometimes lengthy period before you start working.

In Chapter 1, I outlined some of the other classroom positions that could lead to working as a full-time or supply teacher. If you are considering entering the teaching profession, but have not yet qualified or applied to do a PGCE, registering with an agency to work in some capacity in a classroom environment or within a school's administration team might be one route you could take.

Most large agencies now act as recruiters for a wide range of educational posts, including administration assistants, SIMS managers, one-to-one tutors, TAs and cover supervisors, as well as for full-time teaching posts. Several agencies that I have spoken to have said that increasing numbers of, as yet, unqualified personnel are taking up these sorts of positions with the view of later becoming teachers. Such posts give valuable classroom exposure and can help the aspiring teacher (supply or otherwise) to decide in a meaningful and practical way if teaching is for them in the long term.

To have worked in a classroom environment for some time will be of enormous help when you come to apply to a training institution as you will be able to talk with some authority about teaching and education in general at your interview. It will also, of course, have given you an insight into what schools are really like – the day-to-day routines, the pressures of teaching, discipline problems, meetings, reports, assessments, dealing with parents … the list goes on. Many NQTs I have spoken to over the years are, frankly, clueless about such things and appear to have stumbled into teaching for a variety of nebulous reasons. Part of the blame, I feel, lies with university departments and teacher training institutions for ignoring the role of the supply teacher and of giving teaching graduates an unrealistic impression of the day-to-day work of teachers.

Assuming you have submitted all the necessary documentation and have survived the face-to-face interview, you are now ready to start work as a supply teacher. You sit back and wait for the money to roll in. You're not quite at the stage where you are looking at the Ferrari brochures, but it's not far off, you reckon. You go home and wait for the phone to ring! Well, not quite.

The chances are that in the first instance an agency will give you a number of short-term assignments to see how you get on in various schools, where you are best suited and how you conduct yourself 'in the field', so to speak. These assignments might only be daily supply jobs or just a few days at a time. They will probably be fairly unsatisfying at first and you might not be teaching your specialist subject.

You will also start to realise that often supply teachers are isolated and ignored by school staff. After all, you are only there for a day or two. No sense in actually getting to know you! This applies particularly if you are on a short-term assignment, but it can apply also to longer-term assignments. I have known supply teachers who have done a term's work for a school and at the end of it few people actually know their names. It can be a fairly dispiriting job at times.

And, of course, it'll be a month or more before you see any money!

You will want to build your reputation as a reliable, competent, academically able, good all-rounder or subject specialist as soon as possible. By doing this, you are likely to get more work, your reputation will spread among the schools that have employed you and you will be the one they ask for when they need help.

You need to show agencies and schools that you are:

- flexible – prepared to take on any work, anywhere, at short notice if need be;
- reliable – you arrive on time; you do the job to the satisfaction – and beyond – of the school;
- competent in your subject – you demonstrate that you know your subject as well as, if not better than, a full-time teacher, and that you can teach it at whatever level you are asked;
- willing – to take on all types of work, especially the tougher assignments, and 'to go the extra mile' when the need arises.

Stay in contact with the agency if work does not materialise immediately; show you are keen and eager, without being too much of a pest; keep up-to-date through their website and through your consultant. The more enthusiasm you show, the more work you will be offered and the better reputation you will gain with the agency.

Once you have started working, a good agency will monitor your work via feedback from the schools, and any problems, criticisms or suggestions will be relayed to you. Equally, if you have a problem with a school, it is up to you to contact your agency and tell them about it. The reputation of the agency in dealing with problems is just as important as your reputation as a qualified, professional teacher.

A word – or several – of caution

Let's not get too carried away with our love affair with agencies. Not everything in the agency garden is rosy!

When speaking to a number of supply teachers and looking at different forums on the internet it is clear that many supply teachers are anything but happy with the way they are treated by the agency they have signed with.

The grumbles are many and varied and below I have selected a few that seem to be the front runners in the 'I hate agencies' stakes.

Too many agencies; not enough work

One of the most common sources of dissatisfaction with supply agencies is that there are too many of them and not enough work to go round. I suspect there are several reasons for this. First, agencies have proliferated in the past 10 or 15 years, and as I have already pointed out, there are a number of agencies that are simply not competent in placing teachers in schools, or they are placing the 'wrong' teachers in the 'wrong' schools.

Second, the recession has meant that a number of agencies have switched from private sector work to public sector (education and the NHS seem to be the most popular) and thus fill their books with clients (you, the supply teacher) to maintain the illusion of 'being busy'. Then, of course, there's the knotty problem of cover supervisors! More on that one later.

Some agencies will promise the earth and deliver very little and after going through the lengthy process of application, interview, amassing your documentation and so on, you might find yourself with little or no work for some considerable time. Some agencies are admitting that the past few years (2009 onwards) have been very difficult in the labour market. Education, of course, also faces budget cuts and retrenchment over the next few years and it is likely therefore that work will be even more scarce in some areas.

What can you do? Well, one thing I would suggest is to apply to a number of agencies. Some teachers I've spoken to use up to nine different agencies. It is certainly not uncommon to be with two or three. By doing that you are at least spreading your profile far and wide and you therefore stand a better chance of picking up work. However, some agencies have accused teachers who do this of being 'disloyal' and therefore it can be counter-productive.

brilliant tip

Remember also that you might have to nominate one main agency when it comes to tax matters.

In difficult economic times, you might have to be less choosy about where you work and what types of assignments you take on. You might have to make the choice between general supply work and insisting on teaching your specialism; equally, you might have to choose a phase of education (primary or secondary) that is outside your comfort zone.

Keep in touch with your agency; let it know you are still available for work and that you are concerned about the lack of work from it. Insist that it is honest with you about your work prospects. There might be genuine reasons that you are not getting work and you need to know what they are.

Rates of pay

Rates of pay are another main source of complaint. Some supply teachers are finding that they are paid different rates for different postings. It is vital that you check thoroughly with your agency when you first sign up with it what rates of pay you can expect. This should be in writing so that there is no dispute should it come to further action.

If you feel the agency is not being fair with you and it appears not to want to remedy the situation, contact your teachers' union local branch and ask its advice. The main unions have free legal advice and they will be able to sort out your problems or at least point you in the right direction.

Another grumble regarding pay is how much the teacher earns relative to how much the agency charges the individual school. Again, my advice would be to ensure that you know precisely the details of financial arrangements that your agency has with each school you are assigned to. If the agency won't divulge this, try asking the bursar of the school you are in. One way or another, you should be able to find out if you are being 'ripped off'.

Many supply teachers are concerned about late payment and find themselves chasing schools and agencies for their money.

If contacting your agency does not elicit the response you want, try contacting your union or threaten to take the agency to the small claims court. The latter will probably be the last resort, but sometimes you have to do whatever it takes.

The NASUWT survey highlights another problem regarding pay. 'The results of the survey suggested that there was no consistent way that supply teachers' pay was calculated with a high number of respondents advising that they were paid on a daily rate (83%) and on an hourly rate (71%).'

This lack of consistency can affect the supply teacher's income as the hourly rate is likely to be less than the equivalent pro rata daily rate. If you are not certain as to the rate you are being paid, check with your agency or employer.

Other respondents from the survey '… also expressed a number of concerns on pay including the variations that occur between employers in the way their pay is calculated, lack of access to the upper pay scale and pay not being subject to cost of living increases.'

Cover supervisors

The whole question of the advent of cover supervisors is a major cause of disgruntlement among supply teachers. Without doubt, they have made a huge impact on the amount of supply work that is available. Many agencies now recruit cover supervisors and teaching assistants, as well as supply or full-time teachers.

A number of supply teachers are finding that their agency books them for what is essentially cover supervisor work rather than as a qualified, expert classroom practitioner. Obviously from a school's point of view it is advantageous financially to employ a cover supervisor over a fully trained teacher. One school I spoke to told me that a cover supervisor costs them approximately £15,000 for 195 days' work which is the equivalent to 75 days' work for employing a supply teacher. It is also clear that many schools are bending the rules about how much cover a cover supervisor can do and whether or not they should 'teach' while in the classroom. Unfortunately, the guidelines and rules about cover supervisors are vague at best.

brilliant tip

Check carefully with your agency before accepting an assignment that you are in fact being employed as a teacher not as a baby-sitter. Hard though it may be, you should not accept any assignment where you are not being asked to take the role of a fully qualified teacher.

Some supply teachers I spoke to questioned why they bothered to train as teachers in the light of the cover supervisor controversy.

Whom to sign with

Quite a few supply teachers seem to be concerned about how many agencies they should sign up with. As I have suggested above, it can be to your advantage to sign up with several different agencies if you are finding work is difficult to come by. But be aware of the disadvantages too. However, if you are happy with your agency and seem to getting sufficient work, then there might not be a need to change.

I think the main advice here is to check out the agency thoroughly before approaching them. Talk to other supply teachers about their experiences with individual agencies. Internet forums are a good way to do this and the TES has one of the best that I have come across. Go to **www.tes.co.uk** and follow the link to its forum under the Community section.

Questions to ask yourself

1 Do I want to work as a freelance, self-employed supply teacher or work through an agency?

2 Am I aware of the advantages and disadvantages of working for agencies and LA supply pools?

3 Do I know what differentiates a good agency from a bad one?

4 Do I know what documentation I will need when approaching an agency?

5 Do I fulfil the 'Flexible, Reliable, Competent, Willing' criteria?

6 If applying to an agency, am I prepared for the interview and do I know what questions to ask?

 brilliant recap

● Work as a supply teacher can be gained through direct approach to schools, through a local authority supply pool (if one still operates in your area), and through signing up with a recruitment agency.

● Rates of pay vary from agency to agency; only LA supply pools guarantee pay according to scale.

● If you are with an agency, check carefully all the details of your contract, especially rates of pay.

● Do some thorough research before approaching any agency.

● Documentation needs to be in place and up-to-date.

CHAPTER 3

The life of a supply teacher

Picture the scene. It's 7.30 a.m., you are just about to sit down to breakfast, the cat needs feeding, the kids are screaming for their cornflakes ... and your phone rings. It's your agency asking you if you are available for work and, if so, can you get to School X by 8.30?

For any supply teacher this scenario will be familiar. It doesn't happen every day, of course, but at some time during your career, it undoubtedly will. What do you do?

The answer to that obviously depends on your circumstances and how desperate you are for work, but there are a few questions to be asked first of all before you accept any assignment. Don't rush into anything without checking a few details.

Let's assume you are available for work. That does not mean necessarily that you want to take the assignment, of course, but it gives us a starting point.

Questions to ask your agency

1   What type of school am I being sent to (primary, secondary, special, grammar, etc.)?

2   What is its reputation?

3   How far away is it? (Get address and directions from the agency if possible, or access the school's website.)

4   What is the nature of the assignment (subjects to be covered, types and ages of classes to be taught)?

5   What is the timescale of the assignment? (Is it worth travelling 30 miles for a half day's work?)

6   To whom should you report upon arrival at the school?

7   Any special considerations or circumstances that should be divulged? (Is the school under special measures, for example?)

When you have satisfied yourself that the assignment is viable and that you are happy with the answers that you have been given, then make the decision whether or not to accept.

brilliant tip

If you have time, check the school's website first to see if what you have been told matches with what the school would like you to believe. If nothing else, it's useful to know what the school looks like if it's one you have never visited before. But, a word of caution! Not all websites are up-to-date. I recently planned a visit to a local school only to find that it had moved from the site where it had been for a long time to another site about five miles away. Their website had not been updated for four years and I ended up being half an hour late for my appointment.

If you still have doubts about the school and you have the time, you could always look at its Ofsted reports on-line. Go to **www.ofsted.gov.uk** and follow the links. When you have found your school you will get basic information about it as well as a map and you can then access the pdf files on all its Ofsted inspections.

The questions above are particularly relevant if you are being offered a long- or medium-term assignment. If you are going to be at the school for a reasonable amount of time, you need to know what you are getting yourself into. However, don't discount the questions if the assignment is only for a day or two. The better prepared you are before arriving at the job, the better you will be able to understand the nature of the assignment and consequently to cope with it.

If you are new to supply teaching you can easily fall into the trap of accepting whatever comes along just to gain experience and to start earning. It's sensible though to think through each assignment before you accept it. And, of course, you are within your rights to tell your agency that you do not want the 'early call and sudden dash' assignments; that you want some notice before going on an assignment to enable you to prepare adequately. A number of supply colleagues of mine have stipulated to their agencies that they want only medium- or long-term jobs and that they require at least a day's notice before starting. In the end it's up to the individual to decide how they want to work and what sorts of assignments they are willing to accept.

The wise and sensible supply teacher will have their 'travelling office' ready to go at a moment's notice. I will look in more detail at what you should carry with you later in the book, but suffice to say you should be properly equipped with a number of emergency and day-to-day materials. The trouble with supply teaching is that sometimes you just never know what you're dealing with until you get to the school!

brilliant timesaver

If you are lucky enough to have a few days' advance notice, use the time to familiarise yourself with the school through its website and, if possible, go to the school and introduce yourself to the cover manager. As long as you ring beforehand, the cover manager might well go through the induction process with you and give you all the information you need for when you start. This will save a lot of time on your first morning, allowing you to start the real work straight away.

On occasion you might find that the nature of the assignment has changed from when the agency first contacted you to when you arrive at the school to start work. The teacher you were originally due to cover has returned early, but another one from a different department or subject area has gone off sick for a week, for example. If this happens it's worth contacting your agency and letting them know about the changes and checking that the same conditions, such as pay rates, apply. As long as you are happy with any changes, there shouldn't be a problem. Remember, flexibility is one of the key qualities of a good supply teacher! If you are not happy with the situation, you have the right to walk away from the assignment. Finding out that sort of information as early as possible saves a lot of angst.

Arriving at school

If you are on your first assignment, your first day is likely to be one that you will either dread or be excited about. Either way, it will feel like starting school all over again and hoping you don't get your head shoved down the toilet by the big kids in Year 11.

brilliant tip

In the words of a colleague: 'Turn up, look the part, do the job.'

Looking the part is important. You are a professional and you should look and act like one when you are on an assignment. Unless the school has a policy that staff can turn up in jeans and T-shirts, then you should dress smartly and conduct yourself in a professional manner. First impressions are important, as we know, and the impression you create on entering a school for the first time might be a deciding factor if or when they ask you back. Equally, the first impression you get of the school can determine whether or not you want to return.

Induction

You arrive at school, having negotiated the car parking facilities, and you've found the reception area. A school that values its supply teachers will have an induction process set up. This might take the form of a personal introduction and welcome, or the supply teacher being handed a bundle of papers and shown to their classroom. A good school should have a combination of both of these. I know a supply teacher who having arrived at reception was told that he was covering such and such a subject and instructed to find a pupil who would show him to his classroom. To add insult to injury, he was then told that the pupils would tell him what work they were doing and he was left to get on with it.

Needless to say, that was the only time that supply teacher worked for that particular school. Schools that don't treat their supply staff with courtesy and respect will inevitably pay the price in the long run.

So, what should you expect during your induction? The cover manager should be on hand to meet you and to give you all the information that you need to be able to start your assignment. This should comprise a tour of the school including, of course, the room(s) in which you will be teaching. Basic 'housekeeping' points should also be covered – cloakrooms, toilets, dining facilities, tea and coffee procedures at break and lunchtimes, staff working areas, computer facilities (supply teachers should be given temporary log-in information and you should be able to access any areas pertinent to your work), staff smoking facilities and so on.

A vital part of your induction is to have full and detailed information about the classes you are about to cover. The cover manager will probably refer you to the head of department or another member of the department for this. In an ideal world you should know what sorts of levels the classes are working at, the nature of the work being undertaken, what the absent teacher was going on to do with the class and, of course, what work has been set for the class for the first day or two. It is reasonable to expect that the first few days' work has already been set for you. However, if you are on a medium- to long-term assignment, you should expect to be setting your own work after three or four days.

Pupil rewards and sanctions need to be explained. Rewards will vary from school to school and can become quite complicated, with multiple form-filling and entries in pupils' diaries or planners or sticking coloured stars in books. Some schools reward pupils for doing that which they should do anyway, such as attending school! Others reward them for effort, progress, excellence and a multitude of other criteria. In one school, pupils with excellent work are sent to the head with the work and are given a certificate then and there, and their parents immediately informed by phone or text by the head. This proved to be a source of great pride for the pupils.

I've always found the pupils will put you right about these matters fairly readily.

Most schools will have a selection of different forms for sanctions and disciplinary matters, usually depending on the severity of the offence. These, too, can be confusing to start with and if you are not careful you can be overburdened with the bureaucracy of it all. However, it is important to know the basics of the system as you will almost certainly have to use the systems at some stage of your tenure.

Registration procedures should be explained during induction. In these hi-tech days even filling in a register is not as simple as it once was. Some schools have electronic registration procedures that require you to be able to log on to the system and then to be able to navigate your way around it. Fortunately, most schools also have a paper back-up facility for when the system crashes, which it no doubt will when you are there!

Paper handouts

Much of what you might receive in the bundle of documents will expand on or clarify that which you have been told. Some schools have a supply teacher pack with such documents as the school handbook, maps of the school, a range of the various forms you might need (including claim forms and internal timesheets), timetable blanks, staffing list with phone numbers, administration information (who does what in the general office) and so on.

brilliant tip

One very handy tip about induction information – make sure it's up-to-date! Too often information given out in such circumstances can be several years' old. Check with the cover manager first. If it's not up-to-date ask for the latest version of whatever is outdated to be given to you in due course. You might need to talk to a member of staff about an urgent matter only to find they left at the end of the previous year. It happens!

It perhaps becomes clear now why getting the induction procedure out of the way before you start at the school is a good idea. It's time consuming and schools are in full flow from about 8.30 a.m. onwards! Sadly, with the best will in the world, you are not the most important person in the life of the school at that time of day. Many supply teachers I've spoken to like to have a trial day before starting a long-term assignment at the end of which they have a much clearer idea about the school and the nature of the assignment.

Expectations

By now you should be ready to start work. What are your expectations and what is expected of you? These will vary from school to school and the circumstances of your assignment. Some schools will expect you to take on the full range of responsibilities and duties over and above your teaching time, especially if you are on medium- or long-term assignments. These could include acting as form tutor, writing reports and assessments, attending parents' evenings, staff or department meetings, INSET sessions, doing breaktime and lunchtime duties and so on. Other schools might have lower expectations and just simply require you to be in front of your classes keeping things 'ticking over' until the regular member of staff returns.

If you are only in the school for a day or two, then clearly expectations will be different and you might well find that all you are asked to do is cover the lessons, using the pre-written lesson plans, with no other responsibilities required of you.

brilliant tip

Always make sure that you leave notes for the returning teacher, no matter how long or short your stay.

Expectations will depend on who you are in the school, so the following section tries to take into account those of the various interested parties and covers a multitude of circumstances: The main members of staff involved are likely to be:

- the supply teacher,
- the head/deputy head/cover manager,
- the pupils,
- the subject leader/head of department (HoD).

The supply teacher

The supply teacher should expect:

- to be treated with courtesy, friendliness and as a fellow professional by all staff;

- to have appropriate work set by the school (at least for the first day or two if it's a long-term stay) which is readily understandable and contains all the relevant information needed by the supply teacher, or to be given time to prepare if circumstances have prevented the school from doing this;

- to be accorded the same working rights and conditions as a full-time member of staff;

- to be given full information about the assignment (see the previous section on 'Induction');

- to be paid on time according to the agreement between the supply teacher and agency or LA;

- to be given assignments that broadly suit the qualifications, aptitudes and experience of the supply teacher wherever possible;

- to be given access to staffroom facilities on an equal basis with full-time staff members – coffee/tea making, staff workroom, staffroom computer facilities, toilets and cloakrooms, etc.;

- to have the same level of security within the school buildings and grounds as full-time staff members;

- to be shown politeness and courtesy by the pupils;

- not to be put in impossible or difficult situations or ones that endanger the supply teacher or others (e.g. covering practical science lessons without proper insurance or experience);

- to fit in with the daily life and routines of the school;

- to be kept up-to-date with any changes that affect the

assignment (for example, timetable changes, changes of subject(s) to be covered, information about newly arrived pupils to their classes);

- to be kept up-to-date about any actions taken by the school regarding discipline problems after the supply teacher has forwarded them to the HoD or other senior staff;
- to be paid for PPA (planning, preparation and assessment) time;
- to be informed of specialist facilities in the school if you are a disabled teacher (the school should be notified in advance of your arrival in these circumstances);
- to be notified about what is expected of you regarding adherence to principles and practices if your assignment is in a faith school;
- to be supported by colleagues (especially senior colleagues) if you face problems in the classroom or elsewhere in the school;
- to be given full access to any resources necessary for the planning and teaching of your lessons;
- to be given temporary log-in and password information to enable you to access the school's IT network.

The head, deputy head, cover manager

For the sake of brevity I have combined these roles because in many schools the task of booking supply teachers might fall to the deputy head or in smaller schools, the head teacher.

The head, deputy head, cover manager should expect from you:

- that you arrive on time – where humanly possible – and ready to start work;
- that you have with you some basic emergency equipment – pens, pencils, rulers and the like;

- that you understand the broad requirements of the assignment;
- that you will conduct yourself with complete professionalism at all times;
- that you will, to the best of your ability, maintain discipline in the classroom and treat all pupils with respect and courtesy;
- that you will teach in accordance with the requirements of the school or within departmental guidelines;
- that you have good knowledge of your specialist subject(s) and can show mastery of it; that you have knowledge and mastery of all subjects if teaching in a primary school;
- that you are, within reason, willing to cover any subject or class that is required of you by the school;
- that you will act in accordance with school rules and policies;
- that you will do nothing to discredit the school, its staff and pupils no matter how bad your experiences are with the school;
- that you will manage all paperwork pertaining to the assignment (timesheets, etc.);
- that you will be flexible and co-operative with timetable changes and emergency requests that are reasonable and would be asked of a full-time member of staff;
- that you fully prepare, teach and mark work (the latter, if requested by the school);
- that you ask for assistance and advice from senior colleagues if you find yourself in a situation that is beyond your competence or experience.

The pupils

They too will have expectations of you. Most pupils I have taught as a supply teacher expect me to be 'a proper teacher' and to know what I'm doing. Ironically, many of them want their supply teacher to actually teach and not just be a classroom supervisor ... and to keep proper order. Naturally, some will see you as fair game for whatever they can get away with and you have to accept that from time to time this will happen. Their perception of you can change. One supply teacher told me that wearing a 'visitor's badge' labelled him as an outsider and therefore fair game in the eyes of some pupils. By taking off the badge he was just a 'regular teacher' and found life a lot easier.

The pupils expect:

- to be treated with respect and courtesy;
- that you learn their names as soon as possible (if on long-term assignment);
- that lessons are delivered in a competent manner that maintains their concentration, interest and attention;
- that you maintain proper and fair levels of discipline and control;
- that their exercise books, folders, worksheets are looked after and not misplaced;
- that their work is regularly marked or some form feedback given to them (this might depend on the school's requirements of you);
- that you are friendly towards them and take an interest in their lives within and, *where appropriate*, outside school;
- that you demonstrate that you 'mean business' if disciplinary action arises; and that you take appropriate actions if necessary according to the school's policies;
- that you will set work appropriate to their ability level and experience and not just deliver 'fill-in' lessons.

Head of department or subject leader

If you are in a secondary school department for a long stay, the HoD or subject leader will most likely be the person you deal with on a daily basis. Their expectations of you will be very similar to those of the deputy head, head teacher and cover manager, with the following additions that are departmental specific.

The HoD will expect:

- that you are a competent classroom practitioner;
- that you maintain appropriate levels of discipline and control;
- that you teach in accordance with departmental guidelines and policies;
- that you respect and look after any departmental resources that you use, borrow or copy;
- that you look after the classroom furniture and environment;
- that you make full and detailed notes of all lessons taught, assessments completed (if required to do so), resources used, homeworks set and completed;
- that you competently plan and deliver your lessons in accordance with school and national guidelines;
- that you show flexibility and co-operation, especially in emergency or unexpected situations;
- that, where possible, you will go 'the extra mile' to ensure the job is done properly;
- that you will do your best to fit in with the departmental staff, especially if on long-term assignment, attend departmental meetings, training sessions, parents' evenings, etc. if required.

These various levels of expectations set out above look daunting and you might wonder why you bothered to be a supply teacher in the first place if you are expected to be some sort of super-human being. Some supply teachers have told me that they do the job because they see it as an easy – or easier – option than teaching full-time. In terms of the flexibility it affords you and the choices it gives you, that might be so. However, if you are going to be an effective and in-demand supply teacher, you have to accept that you should conduct yourself like any full-time member of staff especially if on a long-term assignment, or that you do the best you can and create a favourable impression if you are in for just a few days or so.

As a former head of faculty and head of sixth form I always told any supply teachers who came my way that I expected them to treat the assignment as if it were a full-time post, particularly if they were going to be with us for a while. As you have seen from the case studies in Chapter 1, I was not prepared to put up with mediocre and second-rate supply staff, but equally I valued and looked after those who were doing a good job for us and performed in accordance with my department's requirements and practices.

brilliant tip

The brutal truth these days is that if you want to secure return work from schools that you enjoy working in and build a reputation as the 'must have' supply teacher, you can't afford to fall below the standards of behaviour and expectations that I have outlined.

You might well behave and conduct yourself in accordance with what you think the school expects from you and in accordance with your own standards, but what the school actually wants from you might be very different. As I've said previously, good schools value their supply staff and do everything to make their tenure productive, positive and mutually advantageous. Unfortunately there are schools that show an attitude of indifference, even hostility, towards their supply teachers. Their attitude seems to be that as long as the classes are appearing to run smoothly, quietly and with the minimum of disruption to the regular staff – especially the senior staff who usually end up sorting out any problems – then everything is fine. I have been told in the past: 'All we need is a hot body in front of the class to keep the little ******* quiet for a day or two.' What schools like this don't care about is the quality of teaching from their supply staff and the pupils' learning.

Day to day

In your day-to-day teaching you should occasionally expect to be visited by the cover manager, HoD or deputy head to see how things are going. Many middle managers (HoDs, etc.) adopt the MBWA (Management by Walking Around) style of management and drop into classes unannounced for 5 or 10 minutes. Whenever I did this – and it was valued by staff and pupils alike as it showed that I was taking an interest in their work and their pupils' progress – I always asked to see lesson plans or notes (not the full blown Ofsted-esque variety) and wandered around the class looking at and talking to the pupils. I made no exception as to whether the teacher was one of our regular staff or a supply teacher. In fact it was often more important to see how the supply staff were performing simply because they were unknown and more vulnerable.

As supply staff you should be prepared for something similar to happen from time to time, so make sure you have appropriate notes and information handy. The work might have been set by someone else, of course, so to some extent you are off the hook. But not so if *you* have set it!

Usually you will find that work set by the absent teacher, or whoever is responsible for setting work for absent colleagues, is satisfactory and gives enough detail for you to be able to conduct the lesson with a good chance of securing some positive learning outcomes for the pupils. But we don't live in a perfect world, do we?

So, what do you do when your so-called lesson plan consists of one sentence, along the lines of: 'Design a poster on volcanoes' or 'Copy notes from Chapter 5 of the text book into your exercise books'. I've even had a lesson plan handed to me that said: 'The kids know what they're doing. They'll get on with it.' In over 30 years of teaching I have never known a class that 'knows what it's doing' and can just 'get on with it' without some recap of the previous lesson at the start and some guidance and pointers as to how to progress. If you are a supply teacher with zero knowledge of what the class has done previously, you have little hope of having a successful lesson. And what about the hapless soul who was away last lesson and hasn't a clue what to do?

You have two choices in these circumstances. One, you write the 'instructions' on the board, give out the books and other resources, shrug your shoulders in disbelief and frustration, tell the class to do their best and work quietly and vow never to return to that school (assuming you get out alive). Alternatively, you use your skills and expertise and make a lesson out of the mess you've been left with.

As a professional, of course, you opt for the second choice. So what can you do to avoid the impending catastrophe?

Let's take the favourite 'useless lesson plan' format – the 'Design a poster ...'. Below are just a few ways you can salvage the situation:

- Start with a brainstorming session to find out what the pupils know about, for example, volcanoes. Is it a new topic for them? Do they have some background information? Have they seen any videos or DVDs about volcanoes? Get some facts and figures and list them on the board. Tell them what *you* know about volcanoes (you might even have visited one); discuss any recent news that might allude to the topic.

- Focus their minds on the purpose and audience for the poster: what should it contain, why is it being produced, to whom is it targeted? I've always found the 'Imagine this is for Year 6 pupils at primary school' strategy to be quite effective in these cases.

- Put some useful subject or topic-related vocabulary (garnered for the pupils, of course) on the board (spelt correctly!).

- Discuss different layout or presentation options, pictures, diagrams, charts, graphs, etc. that might be useful to aid understanding.

- Use available and relevant text books (if you can find them!) and suggest sections the pupils should read, or read it with them.

- Suggest, or elicit for the pupils, some poster title possibilities.

- If you have the time and resources you could always try to find some interactive material for them as well (see Chapter 6 on using the internet).

I'm sure you get the idea by now! Two things you learn very quickly as a supply teacher are to improvise and think on your feet. Many a hopeless situation has been saved by quick thinking.

 **brilliant** activity

Using the example above of the 'Design a poster' lesson, see what you could come up with for some of the following:

- poster on the causes of World War I;

- poster on safety in the science laboratory;

- poster on the use of maths in everyday life;

- poster on how pop music developed from the blues.

Day-to-day routines vary according to the type of school you are in. For example, in a primary school I recently visited the pupils go straight to literacy or numeracy intervention sessions on their arrival at school at 9 a.m. At 10.30 they have assembly, followed by break at 10.45 – a very different regime from a typical secondary school where the day will begin with form/tutor period, registration and maybe once or twice a week, an assembly. As a supply teacher in either primary or secondary sectors you could be asked to participate in any of these routines. Long-term supply teachers can be asked to take on the role of form tutors in secondary schools and so might get involved with planning or delivering an assembly.

The role of form tutor in a secondary school is many and varied. It's certainly more than just ticking the register – or navigating the computerised version. You are counsellor, adviser to and admonisher of recalcitrant pupils, arbitrator of disagreements, collector and interpreter of frequently indecipherable notes brought by pupils, and judge and jury of all manner of situations. If that's what the school expects of you, then make the best of it. It's all good experience, remember.

Tutor or form groups can be vertically or horizontally arranged. Vertical groups comprise a selection of pupils from all years in the school so you might be faced with Year 7s through to Year 13s in the same group. Horizontal arrangements mean that the tutor/form group comprises members of just one year.

As well as the day-to-day routines there are other less common events and routines that you might find yourself involved in. How much you are involved will depend on the school's expectations of you, but you should be prepared to at least offer your services where appropriate. Remember, it's about going the 'extra mile'.

The extra mile

Parents' evenings

If your tenure happens to coincide with a parents' evening and you have been teaching the year or class long enough to know their grades, progress, reports' comments and so on, you could be asked to attend the meeting in place of the absent teacher. It would be advisable to tell parents that you are on supply and that obviously you might not know the pupils as well as their regular teacher. However you'll probably have sufficient information to give the parents to make their trip worthwhile. Experience tells me that most parents will be understanding and appreciative of your efforts. Your subject leader or HoD should make sure that you have all the relevant material at hand and access to the school's IT network (SIMS software, etc.) to be able to get the information you need.

As most parents' meetings are after-school events you should consider your travel options, especially if you have to travel a long distance to the school. Some schools put on a buffet meal so that staff don't have to go home first and then traipse all the way back. You might be lucky to be in one of those schools; if not, it's extra sandwiches or a trip to the nearest café or pub.

brilliant tip

Some supply staff who see parents' evenings as part of their job don't ask to be paid for attending them. Others ask for payment in lieu. It's worth checking with your school or agency to see what the financial implications are for you. Keep a check on the hours you work and claim the extra when you put in your claim form.

Sports days

Summer term assignments might coincide with the school sports day and you could be asked to officiate as timekeeper, crowd control, announcer, organiser of pupils for each event and so on. Provided the weather is nice, it's a pleasant way to spend an afternoon.

Evening events – concerts, plays, etc.

I have known English and Drama specialist supply teachers to be involved with the rehearsals and production of plays and concerts with as much enthusiasm as the regular staff. It becomes a pleasant break from the daily teaching routine and is usually much appreciated by the hard-pressed staff whose responsibility it is to put on these events. As with parents' evenings, check with your school or agency about payment issues.

Educational trips

Most educational trips take place during the school day and if you are asked to accompany staff on one, it is worth giving it serious consideration. Your role will probably be no more than crowd control. Theatre trips and the like are usually evening events and you might not get back to school until quite late at night which might be a determining factor for you. Travel implications and costs will need to be thought about, but if it's possible, do it.

brilliant tip

It is worth checking if there are any insurance or risk assessment implications before signing up to a trip.

Awards ceremonies and speech days

These can be daytime or evening events and your role might simply be to 'be there'. Staff who are not directly involved in the event can be asked to undertake crowd control duties or act as ushers for visitors, etc. If you've been at the school for some time on your assignment it might be a nice way to round off your time there to see the pupils you've taught get their awards, prizes, certificates and so on. I'm sure they will appreciate your presence as well if you've taught them for a long period.

Questions to ask yourself

1 Do you know what to ask your agency or LA when you are given an assignment?

2 Have you familiarised yourself with the school before going on a long-term assignment?

3 Are you aware of what the induction programme should ideally contain?

4 Do you know what the school expects of you before you start the job?

5 Have you been given all the information about the classes and the school when you arrive?

6 Are you familiar with the daily routines and procedures of the school?

7 Are you prepared to go 'the extra mile' to secure a return visit?

brilliant recap

- You might not get much notice of an assignment, so make sure you are fully prepared for whatever comes your way.

- Before you accept an assignment, do some checking.

- Arrive on time where humanly possible.

- Look the part.

- Be aware of what's expected of you.

- Learn the daily routines and keep to them.

CHAPTER 4

It's just a phase I'm going through

You've decided that supply teaching is for you. You've brushed up on your classroom management skills and lesson planning abilities; your 'travelling office' is well stocked, SatNav set and you're ready to go.

Supply teachers will, of course, decide for themselves where they feel most comfortable teaching. However, if you are new to supply work, you might not be aware of all the aspects of working in the various phases of education.

The question now is which phase of education do you want to work in? For which one are you most suited bearing in mind your qualifications and experience?

In this chapter I want to look at the different phases of education for which you might be suited and to clarify some of the advantages and disadvantages of each one. Broadly, the chapter deals with working in:

- the primary sector,
- the secondary sector (including a note on academies),
- special schools,
- secure training centres for young offenders.

You might also get work in colleges or universities. Check with your agency if you are interested in tertiary education.

Working in the primary sector

There is no reason why properly trained and fully qualified teachers cannot work in both primary and secondary phases of education in the UK. However, if you are thinking of transferring from secondary to primary schools, you might be asked to undertake a short induction period to make sure that you are suitable. One school I spoke to runs a two-day trial period for prospective primary supply teachers wishing to transfer from the secondary sector. Some recruitment agencies also run CPD courses for primary supply teachers. A number of secondary schools that I've contacted also require primary-trained teachers to undergo a short training period if transferring to secondary education. If you are employed through an agency, check with it first.

The 'primary' or 'junior' phase includes a number of different sub-sectors:

- primary schools with children aged 5–11 (KS1 and 2);
- infants aged 5–7 (KS1) who then go on to junior school from 7–11 years (KS2);
- first schools with children aged 5–8/9, transferring to middle schools until 12/13, then on to secondary school. (Middle schools in England are deemed to be either primary or secondary schools by the DfE.)

For the purposes of this chapter, most of the information relates to the 5–11 primary school (KS1 and 2).

As a general rule, I think it is fair to say that primary schools demand a lot from their supply staff, probably more than do secondary schools, so be prepared to work hard if you are in this sector.

Advantages of working in the primary sector

One of the main advantages coming out of the research by Hutchins *et al.* (2006) is the greater job satisfaction felt by primary supply teachers compared to that of their secondary colleagues. Much of this is to do with the relative lack of pupil behaviour problems in primary schools, but generally working with younger pupils and having less paperwork to do correlates with a less stressful working environment.

Many supply teachers said that they felt better supported in primary schools, especially by the co-operative planning arrangements with parallel classes. This means that lesson or project planning in a primary school is often easier as it tends to be a shared task.

Primary supply teachers are more likely to be involved in CPD courses, although it has to be said that a well-organised secondary school will also include their supply staff in such courses.

The daily work pattern is likely to be easier – or less problematic – in a primary school as they tend to concentrate on literacy and numeracy requirements in the morning sessions, and much of the planning for these classes will already have been done, thus relieving the supply teacher of another planning burden.

Supply teachers in primary schools are much more likely to teach actively, rather than supervise, another factor affecting job satisfaction rates, and which is why we went into teaching in the first place.

Primary teaching is generally less demanding academically than in a secondary school, but this does not mean that high standards should not be expected.

Younger children tend to be more inquisitive and eager to learn and therefore you can focus rather more on teaching and learning as opposed to behaviour management and the constant battle to keep teenagers on task.

Nationally, primary schools report a shortage of supply teachers for Year 6 and reception/foundation classes. If this is your particular area of expertise you might find yourself in demand as a supply teacher.

Primary supply teachers will normally take the same class for all their lessons during a day and can therefore build up a rapport with the pupils. If you are on a medium- or long-term assignment, this relationship can be advantageous to you in your classroom control, lesson planning and assessments as you will get to know your class well and they will, in turn, trust you if you are any good.

Supply cover is simpler in a primary school because teachers are trained in all aspects of the primary curriculum, whereas in secondary schools the issue of matching expertise to need is more complex.

As with supply work in any sector, you are expected to be independent and to be able to cope by yourself the majority of the time. As a primary school supply teacher you will generally teach the range of subjects, especially if you are on a medium- or long-term assignment. This could include most, if not all, of the following:

- Literacy
- Numeracy
- Science
- RE
- Geography
- History
- Music
- Art
- Design technology
- PE (indoor and outdoor)
- Dance
- Foreign Languages.

brilliant tip

It is advisable to build up your own stock of worksheets and other resources that can be used for the whole age range of the primary/ middle sector. Michael Parry's book *100 Ideas for Primary Supply Teachers* is a great starting point for ideas in all the subject areas in the primary curriculum.

It is an entitlement that all primary school pupils are taught a foreign language, either French, Spanish, German or Italian, and many training institutions offer specialised training courses for primary teachers wishing to teach Modern Foreign Languages (MFL). If you are a supply teacher with MFL training, either in primary or secondary, it will be a useful addition to your CV and will enhance your chances of securing supply work in primary schools.

Disadvantages of working in the primary sector

If you are used to working in the secondary sector you will be expected to cover all areas of the curriculum if you do supply work in a primary school so it's as well to go in armed with a plethora of materials and resources for all ages and abilities.

You should be prepared for more fussy and demanding behaviour, particularly from the youngest pupils who will need more doing for them. They will probably want to know your entire life history in the first morning. Annoying though this might be, it is a good way of creating a rapport with them and getting to know them as individuals. They will also need more supervision when doing certain tasks, particularly in practical subjects like art, or changing to do PE.

You will probably be more involved in the daily routines of school life and be expected to do playground duties (according to Hutchins over 60% of primary schools expect supply teachers to do this), line them up at the start and end of break times and lunch, supervise them over lunch, see them out at the end of the day, and attend assemblies and so on. For primary trained teachers this is normal routine, but if you are more used to working in the secondary sector, it will be a completely different work pattern in a primary school.

On balance, primary supply teachers work longer hours than their secondary counterparts, and are more likely to work in the evenings preparing materials for the next day.

While most secondary cover managers will recruit from agencies or LA supply pools, primary heads generally prefer supply teachers whom they know personally or by word-of-mouth recommendations, and might well use their own supply pool of ex-staff, parents or other contacts. However, there are agencies that specialise in the primary sector as well if you are new to the school or to the primary sector.

brilliant tips

If you are new to the primary phase of education – having worked mostly in secondary schools, for example – you will find your method of delivering lessons need to be modified. Some teachers find that giving instructions by means of a little song or jingle is more effective in the early years than spoken instructions.

Likewise, rather than giving instructions to the whole class, try doing it table by table or even in pairs.

Smaller children like tangible signs of their good behaviour or good work, so a stock of 'good work' stickers or something similar might be part of your 'travelling office' supplies.

Avoid writing copious notes on the board for younger children.

Instead, create simple instruction sheets that can be given to each table group or pairing, along with a verbal explanation from you.

Younger children will be only too glad to help you, so use them to give out books and materials. If you are with the class for a medium- or long-term assignment, you could rotate these tasks to include as many of the pupils as possible.

Find strategies to get their attention. Some primary school teachers use something that will make a loud sound such as a tambourine or whistle. A quieter option is to tell the class that when they see you with your hand raised that is a signal for them to be quiet. They are then to put their hands up to signal they are ready to listen too. It's surprisingly effective and when the pupils get used to it, it works very quickly.

Working in the secondary sector

I think it's fairly true to say that the majority of supply teachers find most of their work in the secondary sector. This includes maintained schools, academies and faith schools. Research undertaken by the London Metropolitan University and University of Glasgow (*Recruitment, Deployment and Management of Supply Teachers in England* by Merryn Hutchins *et al.*, 2006) suggests that there is a big difference in the extent to which supply teachers are used between primary and secondary phases. The researchers found that the number of supply teacher days used in one year was 82 for primaries and 295 for secondary schools. Another factor they isolated was the size of the school. The bigger the school, the greater number of supply teachers are used. The percentage of pupils on free school meals was a factor, and more pertinent, the GCSE results in secondary schools. The researchers found that schools with over 65% of 5A*–C passes used fewer supply teachers than those with figures below this level. The conclusion one draws here is that if you want to work in the secondary phase select a school with high numbers of disadvantaged pupils, poor exam results and lots of kids!

Advantages of working in secondary schools

Working in a secondary school can be stimulating and challenging, and great fun as well. You get to show your expertise in your speciality if your assignment is matched to your training and experience. However, doing general cover can be interesting too. Having taught just about every subject on the timetable over the years I can testify that you learn a great deal about other subjects and the different demands of teaching them. This is all good experience and can add to your armoury of skills. Even when pupils ask you a question you can't answer in a subject that is not your speciality, you can turn that to your advantage by helping the pupils to find answers for themselves and doing it with them. And, of course, pupils like to show their knowledge and skills in various subjects and to share them with the uninitiated supply teacher.

You have a greater number of resources in a secondary school to call upon to help with the planning and delivery of lessons. More facilities are at hand, such as ICT and the library, which will be discussed in Chapter 5.

Unless you are on a long-term assignment, you will probably have less involvement in the daily routines of school life (assemblies, playground duties and so on). This means your working day can be shorter than that of a primary school supply teacher.

As a general rule, placements in a secondary school tend to be longer than in any other phase of education, which allows you to settle in and plan on a longer scale, and to get to know the school, its staff and pupils. Of course, some supply teachers like to move schools on a daily basis, so its advantage might be questionable for those teachers.

Disadvantages of working in secondary schools

The research mentioned above found that the level of job satisfaction was lower in secondary schools, often as a result of pupil behaviour problems. Nearly 29% of supply teachers had turned down work because of poor behaviour in particular schools.

Another factor mentioned was the high proportion of secondary schools that expected the supply teacher simply to supervise pupils doing set work. Research suggests that only 43% of secondary supply staff taught their own specialist subject. Many supply teachers feel this is a de-skilling experience and, as I have intimated already, they much prefer to teach, whether it's a properly pre-planned lesson by the absent teacher or one of their own lessons. I have heard it said that being a supply teacher in a secondary school is akin to the job of a caretaker or a baby-sitter. It would seem therefore that some secondary schools' expectations of supply teachers are sometimes lower than those of the teachers themselves.

If you are on a medium- or long-term assignment in a secondary school you are likely to face a greater marking burden than in any other age phase. This might not be so much of a problem if it's in your specialist subject area, but you could be faced with marking work that is outside your specialism if you are on general cover. Check with your cover manager about the school's policy on marking.

The question of pupil behaviour can be a constant source of concern for supply staff in secondary schools. This, of course, will depend on a number of factors, but schools with low exam results (i.e. poor 5A*–C figures at GCSE) usually experience greater behavioural problems from pupils when supply teachers are brought in, and are the most negative about the impact of supply teachers on pupil behaviour. Your pupil management skills will often be tested in the secondary classroom.

brilliant tip

It is always as well to check carefully on the school's reputation, practices and procedures before accepting any assignment if you have any qualms about your ability to cope with poor behaviour.

Working with adolescents is never easy. You need to bear in mind that at secondary age, pupils can be at their most awkward, rebellious and aggressive, but they can also be at the most vulnerable stage of their lives as well. The impact of broken homes, parental unemployment and poverty can be difficult to appreciate and handle at times, and you need to be very thick skinned, but also sensitive towards pupils with those sorts of problems. As a supply teacher, you could find yourself in the firing line. Always be sympathetic, but never try to 'solve' the problems. Leave that to the staff with pastoral responsibilities.

If you are not used to working in a secondary school, the sheer size of the place and numbers of pupils that you encounter can be off-putting at first. It's more difficult to find your way around a secondary school than, say, a smaller primary school. The majority of the pupils are physically bigger and this can be quite intimidating at first!

Whether the next point is an advantage or disadvantage is debatable, but most secondary schools find it difficult to recruit supply teachers to some practical subjects, such as PE and technology. This point was corroborated by a well-known national recruitment agency I spoke to that added physics and humanities to the list. If these are among your specialities you might find yourself in demand as a supply teacher.

Secondary schools have a higher than average sickness rate among their staff. Some of this is due to stress-related conditions caused by excessive demands made on them by heads, local authorities and government, as well as the problems they face on a daily basis in the classroom, and can be long-term. Without wishing to sound callous and unsympathetic, this might be an advantage to supply staff looking to work on long-term assignments in the secondary sector. However, you might succumb to the same conditions!

Less important disadvantages include:

- working in isolation from other staff, locked away in your own classroom;
- the management of supply staff is more difficult in a secondary school;
- pupil assessment can be complicated and convoluted in secondary schools if you are on long-term assignments;
- secondary supply teachers are less likely to be involved in CPD programmes than are their primary counterparts.

Academies

Although the extension of the academy programme under the coalition government is still relatively new in 2011, it is worth mentioning them from the point of view of the supply teacher. The problem is that there is very little documented evidence about academies and their attitude to supply staff.

Academies are obliged to maintain pay and conditions of service for existing staff when they convert to academy status, but new staff joining the school might not be included in this and could be subject to different pay and conditions. How this applies to supply teachers is not at all clear at the moment.

Theoretically there shouldn't be a problem and supply teachers should find there is no difference between working in an academy compared to a maintained school. However, as academies can set their own pay and conditions, working hours (including weekends) as well as changing the curriculum to suit their intake, there could be some hidden problems for the unsuspecting supply teacher.

Results from a short survey that I conducted in 2011 show some disturbing trends appearing. A number of respondents said:

- It was common knowledge that most academies do not use supply staff and are opting to use cover supervisors and even PGCE trainees to cover absent staff.

- Academies can dictate their own pay rates for supply staff which, of course, are lower than that of agencies or LA supply pools. This could increase as academies group themselves into consortia to buy in services.

- As academies are not bound by national agreements, they can set their own working hours and conditions, and you could find yourself working on a Saturday or working longer hours than maintained school colleagues.

In a paper published by the NUT in March 2011 (*Teachers' Pay and Conditions in Academies*'), the union suggests a number of questions teachers should ask regarding employment in academies. These apply to supply teachers as much as to their full-time colleagues:

- Does the academy follow the School Teachers' Pay and Conditions Document (STPCD) provisions on teachers' pay structures?

- Does the academy follow STPCD provisions on teachers' working times?

- What is the length of lunch breaks for teachers?

- Is there a guaranteed morning or afternoon break?

- What is the practice with regards to weekly meetings? (Applicable if you are on medium- or long-term supply with a school.)

- Is there an entitlement to CPD? (Applicable if you are on medium- or long-term supply.)

Until the situation becomes clearer, my advice, if you are offered an academy assignment, is to check carefully with your agency, local authority supply agency or union about pay and conditions and working hours before accepting it. As always, the school's website should also be consulted to see if there are any problematic areas regarding employment.

brilliant tips

Whatever type of cover you are doing in a secondary school, you will undoubtedly be faced with a wide age and ability range during any one day. Your approach to teaching a new Year 7 class, for example, might be little different from that of teaching Year 6 in a primary school, but vastly different from the way you would approach a top set Year 11 class. There is a big difference between the ability levels, attitudes, behaviour, knowledge and skills of Year 7 compared to Year 11 and beyond.

Set out your stall from lesson one regarding your expectations of behaviour and attitude in the classes you teach. Supply teachers are often regarded as being not proper teachers by secondary pupils and therefore fair game for all manner of unacceptable behaviour. You need to disabuse them of this idea immediately.

Make sure you fully understand the school's practices, policies, rewards and sanctions procedures as early as possible in your assignment.

Get to know the hierarchy in the school. There will always be a member of the senior management team with responsibility for pupil welfare and disciplinary matters, for example. Make it your business to find out who it is and introduce yourself.

Check the school's policy for allowing pupils to leave the room during a lesson for toilet breaks and a thousand and one other

▶

reasons. A session with a peripatetic music teacher half way through your lesson is a favourite excuse to get out of working!

Avoid being the pupils' 'buddy'. You are not. You are their teacher and as such there should be an appropriate professional distance between you and them. That's not to say you can't be polite and friendly towards them, of course.

Never give out your email address, mobile number or any personal information. You could end up being the subject of cyber stalking or find yourself on some chat room of a social network site. I remember a colleague who, with the best of intentions, gave a 'needy' pupil her email address and mobile number. She ended up being stalked by the pupil for a number of years after the girl had left school.

Working in special schools

While cross-phase teaching between primary and secondary is fairly common, special school teaching is much more specialised and far less common for the average supply teacher. However, it is not impossible that you might be offered a special school assignment.

Special schools are those that are geared to the needs of children with a multitude of severe learning or physical disabilities, as opposed to the special educational needs of mainstream pupils. Teaching in special schools calls for certain skills and training. They are often very challenging but also very rewarding.

Special schools cover a wide range of special educational needs including conditions such as Asperger syndrome, autism, physical disability, neurological dysfunction, Down's syndrome, cerebral palsy, behavioural problems, emotional problems, sight and hearing problems, language and communication needs and so on. Special schools will also cover the normal age ranges that you would find elsewhere. They can be situated on the site of a mainstream school or on a separate site and vary from full board residential to day schools.

> ### brilliant tip
>
> Most individual schools will specialise in a selected range of needs, and it would be advisable to check on what these are before accepting an assignment.

Research would indicate that the majority (72%) of supply teachers working in special schools have been trained for that phase of education, and most special schools will request that potential supply staff are specifically trained in that phase if they are recruiting through an agency. There are a number of agencies that have consultants for special schools and they should be able to advise you as to your suitability.

It is more likely, however, that special schools will have their own pool of known supply staff from which they choose, and they might also do their own vetting of supply teachers. Some special schools train their own supply staff and might ask you to attend a number of days' training, possible unpaid, prior to engagement.

Unlike primary and secondary teaching, you will almost certainly find that you are one of a team in the classroom, aided by at least one TA. You could find yourself working alongside specialist staff, such as speech or occupational therapists.

Working in a special school requires a range of skills that are perhaps outside your normal teaching practice, such as:

● having immense patience with pupils who might struggle with the most basic of tasks;

- being able to understand and appreciate the special need(s) of each pupil;

- the ability to work in a co-operative environment with other non-teaching professionals;

- being able to handle situations, such as violent physical or emotional outbursts by the pupils, and to understand the reasons for them;

- to appreciate and work with pupils' behaviour patterns that might be strange or unknown to you.

Although your first day or two in any school will be strange when you might feel like an outsider with the pupils and staff wondering who you are, this feeling might well be exacerbated in a special school. Pupils will probably not deal with change quite so easily and will look to their TAs or cover supervisors for extra support and guidance, increasing your sense of isolation until they have fully accepted you.

In many special schools the work is not as curriculum driven as it is in other phases of education, and much of your time will be spent on reinforcing specific social skills of the pupils, rather than the more traditional academic work you would be expected to undertake in a primary or secondary school. This might involve much more of a practical, 'hands-on' approach such as using role play and circle time activities, keeping lessons moving to reduce behaviour problems and dealing with the often short attention span of pupils with special needs.

Having said that, you could find yourself covering a Sixth Form or GCSE lesson in a special school where your academic prowess is called upon.

Teaching science in a special school

The point has already been made elsewhere that unless you are a qualified and preferably an experienced science teacher, you should not be asked to cover science lessons in any school, regardless of which phase it's in. However, let's assume you are a qualified science teacher and are asked to cover science in a special school, what do you need to be aware of?

In 'Teaching Science to Pupils with Special Needs' (2000), Peter Borrows highlights some of the problems associated with teaching science to special needs pupils. The main consideration is the balance between entitlement of special needs pupils to science and the potential dangers to themselves and to others when they are in a science environment.

As a supply teacher, you might not be fully aware of the special needs of an individual pupil or fully understand the health and safety implications. Borrows suggests a number of factors that need to be taken into account. Below is a short summary of these:

- Convey important safety messages orally so that non-readers, partially sighted or dyslexic pupils are included.
- Visually impaired pupils will work with science equipment much closer to their faces than mainstream pupils. This can be particularly dangerous if handling chemicals or hot substances and they will need to wear lab goggles.
- Pupils with motor control difficulties are more likely to splash chemicals and will thus need to have full face or body protection.
- Pupils in wheelchairs will not be able to move out of the way quickly if something goes wrong and will need extra protective clothing, such as a pvc apron.
- Very disturbed pupils might use some equipment as a weapon against other pupils or the teacher and should therefore be given extra supervision by other adults, such as a TA.
- Schools with emotionally and behaviourally disturbed pupils

will face specific problems as the pupils are more likely to lose control at some time or another, with potentially very dangerous consequences for all concerned.

The above points will have implications on how you plan and deliver your lessons, what activities you deem to be safe, the risk assessment you undertake and how you use the classroom support to best effect. It would be as well to bear some of these points in mind if you are teaching other practical subjects in a special school. Departmental schemes of work in a secondary special school should identify the high risk activities and it is important that you have access to these from the start.

The stresses associated with working in a special school compared to a mainstream school

Conventional wisdom would suggest that working in a special school is more stressful than working in a mainstream school. After all, you could be dealing with emotionally disturbed or physically violent pupils. Research indicates that, on the contrary, special school teachers face no more stress than their mainstream counterparts. The only difference is the source of stress.

The main causes of stress in mainstream schools appear to come from the following:

- noisy pupils;
- lack of time to spend with individual pupils;
- Ofsted;
- pupils' poor attitude to work.

I don't think any of these will come as a surprise to any teacher.

In special schools the main source of stress appears to be shortages of equipment. This is somewhat surprising as one might have expected special schools to be better resourced than mainstream primary or secondary schools. One suggestion is that special school teachers feel that they lack the equipment to deal with the range of pupils and the diversity of their particular needs.

The following testimony from one respondent in a survey by Michelle Williams and Irvine Gersch's in 2004 is fairly typical of the way many new teachers feel about their first job and the stresses that teachers face day to day:

During my NQT year I felt 100 times more stress working in a mainstream school. This was due to the pressure of having 35 children in my class; no learning support assistant help; and not receiving sufficient support in school from either school colleagues or headteacher. I was off sick for half a term with stress and considered giving up completely. ***Working now in a special school is much nicer and less stressful.***

(Quoted from an article by Michelle Williams and Irvine Gersch in *British Journal of Special Education*, 2004)

Working with young offenders

In late 2010 I was working in a school with two other supply teachers, one of whom I know well, the other I'd met on a few occasions. During a lunch time chat, both of them quite independently told me that they had worked in young offenders secure units as supply teachers. It was an area of supply work that I had not previously considered and was surprised when they both said how much they'd enjoyed the work.

While it is unlikely that you will be offered an assignment in a secure unit, if there is one in your geographical area, it could be a possibility. As with special schools, the skills you need as a supply teacher in a secure unit might be different from the ones you employ in mainstream teaching. For one thing, the ability levels of many of the pupils will be considerably lower than in a mainstream school and there will be an emphasis on basic skills, literacy and numeracy and more practical subjects.

According to Direct.gov.uk there are three types of accommodation for young people in custody:

- a young offenders institution – run by the prison service for young offenders aged between 15–17;
- a secure training centre – accommodation for offenders up to age 17 that provides education and vocational training;
- a local authority secure children's home – run by local authorities to accommodate the most vulnerable young offenders.

All of these will have programmes of education and training and the youngsters will spend some of their time in the classroom, as well as time for sport and fitness training.

As there is little official documented evidence about working as a tutor or supply teacher in a secure training centre, much of what follows is based on interviews with and experiences of supply teachers who have spent some time working in these units.

As background to what follows, it's worth knowing a few statistics that are relevant and should inform your decision to work in a secure unit or your planning of lessons for such an assignment. In a study done by Chitasbesan et al. (2006) into the mental health needs of young offenders in custody, the researchers found that 36% of their sample of some 301 youngsters had an education/work need; 31% had a mental health need; and 48% had a social relationship need. Some 20% had an IQ of less than 70, which actually meets the criteria for learning disability. The mean reading age was 11.3 years, which was significantly lower than their average chronological age of 15.7 years, and has important consequences in lesson planning where any extended reading skills are needed.

It perhaps goes without saying that many of the young people in such environments have had fairly negative experiences of mainstream education, with a high proportion having failed to complete compulsory schooling and thus have ended up without any educational qualifications. Many of the pupils in these units might therefore display a reluctance to learn or be taught in the traditional way, will probably show short attention spans, have low self-esteem and will switch off unless the work is of intrinsic interest to them.

The evidence points to the fact that they tend to respond better to work which has vocational or practical slant or which is based on real-life situations. Courses such as plumbing, cooking, mechanics and bricklaying seemed to be favourite vocational courses, whereas the more academic subjects were less well received by the pupils.

One supply teacher I spoke to had taught art in a secure unit and told me that the pupils were more interested in 'making things' rather than drawing or painting. She had made a large papier mâché dragon with some younger pupils, which had been a successful project but she had been surprised by the short attention span and lack of self-esteem of many of them.

There were safety issues about the use of some materials used in art (for example, scissors, wire, oil or acrylic paints) and she recommended that 'softer' materials, such as paper (for origami and paper sculptures) and felt (for sewing or soft toy construction) are safer options. It is recommended that the supply teacher keeps a very strict eye on what is being used and makes sure that materials are counted out at the start and counted in at the end of each lesson.

Other art suggestions mentioned were:

- tie dyeing,
- tattoo designs,

- 'glass' painting on acetate or clear polypockets,
- sewing (popular with boys, apparently),
- straw sculpture and modelling,
- greeting cards design (Mother's Day was particularly popular),
- graffiti art.

Internet access might be restricted or even banned in some units, so planning lessons with an IT component could be problematic. As a result it might not be advisable to plan your lesson on a memory stick as you might not be allowed to take one into the unit.

brilliant tip

Another supply teacher said, 'Think simple, practical, hands-on, instant results. Think about getting numeracy and literacy subtly into their work, such as measuring and weighing or designing and creating posters and so on.'

A third said, 'I've done quite a lot of long-term supply in a secure unit. I loved it, and it was much easier than a special school ...'

The following points came out of extensive interviews with two colleagues who have worked in secure units on many occasions. Both said that it was an enjoyable experience, but agreed that it doesn't suit everybody. In the places they worked, the trainees (as the inmates are correctly known) are on first name terms with their regular staff. This might not sit comfortably with supply staff and could lead to tension if you prefer a more formal relationship.

They reported that there was little difference in the curriculum but standards were much lower, as the research above has supported. There is a great emphasis on basic skills, functional literacy and numeracy, and lesson planning should take account of this. You will probably find yourself teaching all subjects as you would in a primary school.

Ability levels vary, but the groups are always much smaller than you would find in a school and therefore you can get to know the trainees better and respond to them on an individual basis. There is, however, a tendency towards a greater turnover in trainees than you would normally come across as they are discharged and new ones appear.

Routines are fixed and controlled by the staff and generally discipline is not a problem for teachers as unit staff are always present, both in and out of the classroom. All doors are locked and this can be quite claustrophobic and intimidating at first. None of the supply staff said they felt in any danger from the trainees since they are in a secure environment and there are plenty of systems in place to avoid problems. The staff monitored each trainee carefully and would, for example, accompany them to the toilet mid-lesson. They would also remove any trainee from a class if there were discipline problems or the possibility of a violent outburst, and take them to an isolation room.

One colleague mentioned that he had been given some basic training in passive techniques at the start of his assignment for 'fending off unwanted attention' by the trainees.

Because the classes are smaller than you would find in a school, and the number of staff proportionately greater, the resources tended to be more generous in terms of equipment and staff.

The working day might be slightly longer than you would expect in a school, and because trainees do not have the same sorts of holidays as school pupils, there is the opportunity to work more days if you want.

Summary

As you can see, the choices before you as a supply teacher are very varied and interesting, allowing you to work with pupils of all ages, backgrounds and academic abilities. The wider you spread your net, the more experience you will get and this can only be of benefit to you in your career as a supply teacher. To be able to show that you have worked in more than one phase of education, with the range of pupils and everything that entails, will look impressive on your CV if your aim is to secure a permanent post.

brilliant recap

- Decide which phase you are most suited for based on training, prior experience, qualifications and interests.

- Consider the advantages and disadvantages of each phase before making a decision.

- Cross-phase teaching is possible, but be aware of extra training implications if you are transferring.

- As well as the main sectors mentioned in this chapter, you could get supply work in colleges or universities.

- Always check with your agency if you are offered supply work outside of your regular 'comfort zone' phase.

- If you are offered work in a faith school, it is no longer legally required that you belong to that particular faith, as long as you show respect for it.

CHAPTER 5

Lesson planning

Jim Smith in his book *The Lazy Teacher's Handbook* says, 'At the heart of every lesson you won't find the PC, the projector, the interactive whiteboard, worksheets ... You won't even find a teacher. You will find the students.'

In your desire to be the 'must have' supply teacher, you will want to show that you are an excellent planner of lessons as well as being able to deliver the 'killer lesson'. When all is said and done, it's all about the kids!

In my experience, one of the hardest parts of a teacher's job is to get the lesson planning right, especially if your lesson is being observed. Good supply teachers put in as much effort to their planning as do their full-time counterparts, particularly if on a long-term assignment. There might well be times, of course, when the planning is done for you by the absent teacher or someone designated by the HoD or deputy head, in which case you are at the mercy of someone else's efforts. As we have seen in Chapter 3, they are not always up to the mark!

Supply teachers tend to be faced with three main lesson scenarios:

- the unplanned, emergency lesson that has been thrust upon you unexpectedly;
- the pre-planned lesson by the absent teacher;
- the planned lesson done by you when on medium- or long-term assignment.

Each one of these types presents different problems and difficulties, especially when you have little time or scant background knowledge of the class. However, with some basic lesson planning knowledge and a bit of forethought, these can be overcome. I will deal with each of these in turn and introduce a few new ideas into the lesson planning process.

The unplanned, emergency lesson

This is the least likely eventuality faced by supply teachers, but it does occur and when it does you need to be ready for it. This type of lesson can be categorised as the one-off, emergency, unplanned, straight-off-the-top-of-your-head variety. It might occur if someone suddenly goes home ill, or has simply forgotten to leave any lesson notes for you. It doesn't require too much effort on your part and the aim is to keep the class engaged in some relevant, meaningful activity for an hour or until you can find the HoD or deputy head to acquire some lesson material.

It goes something like this. You are sitting in the staffroom finishing your sandwiches and looking forward to that free period on your timetable immediately after lunch. Technically, it's your PPA time, but actually you have nothing much to do. The cover manager enters and heads straight towards you. Immediately the approaching hurricane/earthquake sensors spring into action and your first inclination is one of flight. However, you are a brave soul and stay put.

Cover manager: You've got a free after lunch!

You: (guardedly) Yes.

Cover manager: Could you do me a big favour?

Here it comes!

Cover manager: Mrs Y has just gone home sick and I've got

nobody else available to cover her class. It's a nice little Year 8 history group. Could you do it for me?

You: Did she leave any work?

Cover manager: No, sorry. Can I leave it with you?

You: (being the cooperative, flexible, 'going the extra mile' type) Yeah … OK.

You could, of course, have said no, but you enjoy working at this school and would like to get asked back. There's one thing that cover managers, deputy heads and heads dislike most of all – seeing a supply teacher sitting around with nothing to do!

Your next move? You might have with you your memory stick filled with emergency lesson ideas that you've laboriously put together on those days when you weren't working and so you head for the nearest computer. Switch on, plug in, print off! Next stop, photocopier, and job done.

Oh, if it were only that easy! However, it doesn't have to be such a problem. Remember, in these circumstances you are not expected to produce a full-blown lesson plan, simply to keep a class occupied with some relevant work … and it's not difficult to get some generic lesson ideas together quickly.

If it's possible at short notice to book a computer room, even better, but let's assume that all you've got to work with is a set of history books that the class has been using.

After getting the class seated, explaining who you are and why you are there, ask them what topic they've been studying in their history lessons. Let's say, for the sake of argument, it's the First World War.

I've detailed below some quick, cheap and cheerful lesson ideas that work with a variety of subjects, particularly English, history, geography, PSHE and the like, and require little or no planning by you. Most of these will work with primary or secondary pupils, but might need a bit of differentiating depending on age and ability levels.

 **activities**

Subject word

Write the subject word on the board: H-I-S-T-O-R-Y

The pupils have to come up with a word for each letter of the title that is relevant to the topic they are studying. These can be people, places or objects. So, for example:

> H – Haig, General (person)
>
> T – trenches (place)
>
> Y – Ypres (place)
>
> R – rifles (objects)
>
> … and so on.

Using the available resources – text books, their own exercise books and computers (if available) – they choose one or two of these headings and research them, making notes in their books or on paper. This can be a timed exercise, leaving opportunities for the class to feed back their findings to their classmates at the end. They can swap ideas as well and there can be a prize for the pupils who have managed to find a relevant word for every letter of the subject name.

Beginnings and endings

Especially useful for English, history, PSHE and geography lessons.

Put pupils into pairs. Give each pupil a sheet of A4 paper. Ask them to think up an idea for a story based on a topic they have been studying. Let's say it's a PSHE lesson on bullying.

On the paper, they have to write no more than six lines of the beginning of a story on bullying. On the bottom of the page, they have to write no more than six lines of the ending to their story. When they have completed this, they swap papers and their partner has to write the middle of the story without any communication with the other person. The trick here is to ensure that sufficient information is given at the start of the story for the partner to be able to carry it on to the end, and to dovetail the middle with the ending that has already been written. It's not as easy as it first appears, but is a great way to get pupils to understand some basics of narrative writing and to keep them engaged for an hour, as well as exploring in a creative way some of the issues raised in the topic.

Storyboards

Find out the topic they have been studying. For example, a geography lesson on the Kobe earthquake in Japan. Set the scene for them. Imagine an ordinary Japanese family caught up in the earthquake. Ask the class to storyboard a scene or an episode about this family, from the first indications that something is not right (the first rumblings and shaking of the house) to the full-on earthquake hitting their street.

The storyboard need only be six to eight frames (a piece of plain A4 will do for this) and stress that they don't have to be brilliant artists to do it. Remind them that what goes on in the background of each frame is just as important as what is happening in the foreground. They can add a caption or speech bubbles to each frame if they wish, but essentially the pictures should tell the story. If coloured pens are available, let them use these as well.

Crossword puzzles

Useful for just about every subject.

Pupils to create a crossword in which all the clues must be based on the topic they have been studying. Using A4 paper, draw a square of between 8cm and 12cm depending on how big they want the puzzle to be. Create the crossword grid and number the across and down squares. Believe it or not, this will probably be the most difficult part of the whole procedure. All the clues must be related to the topic – they can be straightforward factual clues, anagrams or cryptic clues. Answers can go on a separate sheet, and when they've finished they can swap crosswords with their partner.

▶

This is also a good exercise to bring in differentiation as it can be adapted to all levels of ability. Some of the slower, less able pupils might like to do just a small crossword or a wordsearch, whereas some of the faster, brighter ones will like the challenge of creating something a bit more sophisticated and demanding.

Your survival kit will no doubt come in handy for this type of lesson as pupils soon realise that rulers and pencils can be quite handy.

What if …?

Ask pupils to speculate on various scenarios, all beginning with the question, What if …? Here are some examples:

- What if we lived in an earthquake zone? How would our lives be affected?
- What if the Germans had won the First World War? What would Europe be like today?
- What if money didn't exist? How would we manage?
- What if there's life on Mars? What would it be like?
- What if it stopped raining forever?
- What if the sun went out?

The short cut to this lesson is to ask the pupils to come up with their 'What if …?' questions. They will undoubtedly be more inventive and fun than anything you can think up. However, what they do is to open the door to some interesting discussions and debates after the class has moved on from the obvious one-thought answer. This lesson can be done in table groups, pairs or, if you're feeling really brave, a whole-class debate. It lends itself to written or oral work. With a GCSE group it might also contribute to their Speaking and Listening grade in English.

Of course, all of the above can be used at any time in any lesson situation, but they are suitable ideas for the emergency lesson where minimal planning and preparation is required. And imagine how impressed your HoD (assuming Mrs Y isn't the

HoD) will be when they find out that the class has had a great lesson and they haven't had to spend time finding work for you and planning a lesson in the five minutes before the bell rings.

The pre-planned lesson by the absent teacher

Most of the time, your work as supply teacher will involve delivering the pre-planned lesson created by the absent teacher or some other designated person. Theoretically, this should be the easiest option of the three – you don't have to put in any planning effort, the lesson notes should be self-explanatory and all you have to do is go in and deliver it to a group of fresh-faced youngsters desperate for your extensive knowledge and pedagogical brilliance. But as we have seen already, life is rarely like that.

There are three scenarios you could be faced with here:

- the under-planned, one-line lesson: 'Design a poster on volcanoes' (had this one a number of times!);
- the over-planned, page after page of notes, suggestions, ideas, extension work, homework, kids-to-look-out-for and so on that takes half the lesson to digest;
- the well-planned, concise, sufficiently detailed plan written by an experienced and competent teacher who also appreciates your position as a supply teacher.

It is to be hoped that you have the third one in front of you, but don't rely on that fact. Too much information is as bad as too little and can lead to your having to do a lot of preparatory work to fill the gaping chasms in the lesson plan, or requiring the whole of the lesson beforehand to assimilate it all.

Ideally, what you need for a pre-planned lesson is:

- an indication of lesson objective(s) and learning outcomes;
- a concise account of the work to be undertaken, preferably in bullet points (page or chapter references included);

- an indication of the type of class – year and ability level;
- if any other adult will be present (TAs);
- indication of homework assignments, with handing-in date;
- a contact name if things go wrong;
- extension work – a few short suggestions;
- room number.

All other information should be given to you on separate sheets, such as worksheets, seating plans, register, etc.

A quick warning note about seating plans. Most schools have some form of seating plan policy that is based on a number of parameters – boy-girl, boy-girl; alphabetical order by surname; table groups based on ability; ability pairings, and so forth – and it's as well to keep to the school's rules on this assuming you are supplied with a plan in the lesson notes. However, seating plans can create as many problems for teachers as uniform issues. Many seating plans I've been given when working as a supply teacher are out-of-date and thus of little use. It's also questionable just how effective they are anyway, and the rationale behind them.

brilliant tip

Always make a point of writing some notes at the end of the lesson for the returning teacher so that they know what you have done and how far the class has got in the work set, along with any homework requirements. You should also make notes about any pupils who have been particularly troublesome and any action you have taken about their behaviour, as well as, of course, mentioning pupils who did exceptionally well and who are deserving of merits or whatever the school gives as a reward for good work.

The majority of lessons planned by the absent teacher will be paper-based, unless you are covering IT lessons. IT teachers do everything on-line. IT teachers assume that everyone else knows all the software inside out and back to front. IT teachers find it difficult to conceive that the rest of us mere mortals are not necessarily *au fait* with web design and animation techniques, spreadsheets and databases. As a result IT teachers rarely, if ever, leave a paper-based alternative in case – and it will happen – the whole network crashes while you, the supply teacher, are in control.

brilliant tip

Always ask if there's a plan B should there be a technological meltdown. Frequently, there isn't! Logically, there should be.

PE teachers are another group whose lessons are rarely planned with the supply teacher in mind. What do you do with: 'Pupils to play five-a-side football' as a lesson plan? For one thing you will *never* have a group that has exact multiples of five in it and so you will end up with 5 v 4 or 6 v 7 or some other combination – you do the maths! – to a querulous chorus of 'It's not fair, sir!' Add in the several who have forgotten their kit, feel ill, have been sick at break, have a broken arm or a stubbed toe, or whose mum has said he can't do PE today because 'he's had diarrhoea through a hole in his shoe', and your – or their – nice neat little lesson plan is blown out of the water. And don't get me started on the interpretation of the rules of five-a-side.

Other traps to be aware of

- 'We did this work last lesson, sir.' Sometimes a ploy to get out of doing anything or to make your life difficult, but not necessarily. Check their exercise books for proof.

- The class has just started a new topic and has had only one lesson on it so far. Your – and their – knowledge is minimal.

- Reference made to text books that are nowhere to be found. 'We usually borrow them from Miss B, sir.' And of course Miss B is using them this lesson!

- Computer, video and DVD- based lessons:

  - the system crashes;

  - you have no log-in password or user name given to you at induction;

  - you can't get the DVD to play or any sound out of the speakers;

  - the blackout blinds are broken and it's a bright sunny day and no-one can see the screen.

- Relevant resources have not been left for you – felt tip pens, sugar paper, scissors, etc.

It is unlikely that you will be asked to cover practical lessons unless you are qualified and experienced in the particular subject, but forewarned is forearmed.

- **Science** – unless you are a qualified and experienced science teacher, you should not be asked to cover a science practical lesson. There are insurance issues to take into account and it is illegal to send supply teachers to do science unless qualified.

- **Drama** – not usually a problem, but be aware of the potential for accidents when pupils are running around on the stage or hall floor, acting mock fights or using 'props' that could injure them; be prepared for a lot of noise.

- **D and T** – again, be aware of the potential for accidents if the lessons involve the use of chisels, hammers and saws.

- **PE** – for indoor or outdoor lessons, make sure at the very least that you wear trainers for your own safety. There are gender issues to be considered here as well. Male supply teachers should not be asked to cover girls' PE and vice versa.

The planned lesson created by the supply teacher

Notwithstanding the amount of work it entails, many supply teachers much prefer to plan their own lessons. By doing so you are in control of the content, objectives, starter and plenary activities and the period of time it will take to deliver. If you are on a medium- or long-term assignment you will be expected to do this anyway. Good supply teachers put in as much effort to their planning as their full-time counterparts and it will be worth all the effort in the long run.

Lesson planning is not always easy and it can be time-consuming, but it is one of the most important parts of your work and needs to be done properly. Without doubt, some classroom management problems that teachers face are the direct result of poor planning as pupils begin to get bored or restless when they have little or nothing that challenges them and keeps them engaged.

If you are being observed, either by the senior management team or by Ofsted, a number of aspects of your lessons will form the focus of the observation. Some of the favourites are:

- challenge,
- variety,
- feedback and assessment.

brilliant tip

When you are planning your lessons it is worth keeping these points in mind. Ask yourself: is the work challenging? Does it stretch all the pupils, no matter what their ability level? Is there sufficient

▶

variety in the lesson? Do I have a stimulating starter activity? Is there the opportunity for both written and oral work? Is there scope for paired, small group or whole class work? Have I considered different learning styles? How will I handle feedback? Can I incorporate it in the plenary session? Is it pupil-pupil or teacher-pupil feedback? Written or oral? How am I going to assess the work and feed this back to the pupils? Peer assessment or teacher assessment?

Lesson planning

Telling someone that their lessons are poorly planned is as upsetting to them as telling them they have an underarm odour problem or bad breath. Seriously, I have seen teachers in tears after an observation feedback session when they have been told that they must improve their lesson planning in order to achieve their objectives, achieve better exam results, engage the pupils more effectively, and thus make the school look better in the eyes of the general public and Ofsted. Like marking, lesson planning is a side of our professional life we least like doing, but is in fact absolutely essential if we are going to be effective in the classroom.

Many teachers will tell you that they don't plan lessons. Don't believe them. They do. They will often point to their head and claim it's all up there, stored away in the memory banks. It might be so, but they still plan their lessons. Whether they do it effectively is another matter!

Effective lesson planning

What makes this aspect of your professional work so important and emotive? Just think of the times when you have planned a brilliant lesson, delivered it with skill and creativity and had it received with enthusiasm and attentiveness by the pupils. Remember how good it felt? Alternatively, remember how desperate you felt when you failed to plan properly and the lesson fell apart with the pupils sitting there looking bored and indifferent, or worse?

Lesson planning is at the heart of what we do as teachers. After all, as Jim Smith said, the pupils are the most important thing and they deserve well planned, skilfully executed lessons.

As part of your induction process at the start of a medium- or long-term assignment, you might have met the HoD, deputy head or second in department and discussed the work they want you to do and the resources available to you from the department or school. Included in these should be the department's or school's schemes of work, the starting point for your lesson planning after the first day or two.

Schemes of work set out in detail the work to be undertaken by a particular year or group of pupils on a particular topic or area of study over the course of a term or half term. While they are not necessarily cast in stone, they should provide you with a week-by-week study guide that allows you to think ahead and which can then inform your lesson planning. As a supply teacher you will not be asked to write schemes of work, although I have known some to do this voluntarily (see the case studies in Chapter 1).

Questions to ask yourself when lesson planning:

- What do I hope the pupils will learn from this topic?
- What can I do to ensure they learn everything that is required by the scheme of work or exam syllabus?
- How will I know when they have?

Starting points

Learn to think like a pupil. All pupils approach lessons and the various topics they include in different ways. Some learn quickly; others take more time. Some like the hands-on approach, while others are more comfortable with the book-based, copious notes style. Not all of them will be interested in every aspect of the topic.

Their regular teacher will know their classes and should take these different approaches into account in their lesson planning. As a supply teacher, you will not necessarily know all this information about the classes you are covering and are therefore at a disadvantage at the beginning. You might, therefore, need to do some investigation to find out what's what.

Consider the following questions as a way of starting to think about your lesson planning:

● What do they already know about ...?
● What do they need to know about ...?
● How can I show or help them to find out about ...?
● What skills will they require in order to do this?

Developing planning from previous lessons

As a supply teacher you will not necessarily have been present at their previous lessons and will have little or no idea about what they have done so far, or how well they have got on with the topic. A good HoD or deputy head will fill in some of the gaps for you, but might not have a detailed knowledge of this particular class.

One way to start, therefore, is to find out exactly what pupils know, remembered or did, and use this as a basis for your lesson planning. The pupils will then have a context for your lessons, rather than being presented with a series of one-off, ad hoc, disconnected lessons.

Try to involve as many pupils as possible in this exercise. One way you could do this is by a well-thought-out Q&A session. Questioning techniques should be constructed carefully, rather than the 'Can you tell me what you did last lesson?' type.

Blooms Taxonomy

Applying some of the aspects of Blooms Taxonomy can provide you with more useful questioning techniques and can result in giving you important information about pupils' knowledge, ability, comprehension and analytical skills. Blooms Taxonomy is constructed in six main categories with the following samples of question tags which you can use to elicit the information you need:

1 Knowledge – list, define, tell, describe, name, who, when, where.

2 Comprehension – summarise, describe, distinguish, discuss, predict.

3 Application – illustrate, classify, show, complete.

4 Analysis – explain, connect, compare, arrange, analyse.

5 Synthesis – rearrange, substitute, generalise, rewrite, what if?

6 Evaluate – prioritise, discuss, choose, decide, determine.

With skilful use of these, you might be able to construct an entire lesson just finding out what the pupils know and where they are in their study of the topic and thus where you are going to take them over the next few lessons. The various categories of Blooms Taxonomy lend themselves to written and oral contributions and can be challenging for the pupils. The resulting information will help you plan the next group of lessons with some certainty as to the ability and progress of the class.

Starter activities can be used to find out prior knowledge and could include:

- pupils writing key words and ideas about the topic on the board;

- timed competitions (allow no more than five minutes) between pupils to see who can remember the most about the topic;

- writing at least five things they know about the topic;

- a simple, quick cloze exercise related to the topic. This would need to be prepared before the lesson, however.

You are now in the position to start planning effectively.

Lesson objectives

If you are planning a series of lessons, you need to be clear about lesson objectives:

- for each lesson;

- where each lesson fits into the scheme of work;

- how the lesson will progress so that objectives can be realised;

- materials and resources to be employed;

- assessment and feedback during and at the end of each lesson.

Lesson objectives state what the pupils should have achieved at the end of the lesson. They can be stated thus: *By the end of the lesson, pupils will be able to ...* (followed by an active verb, for example *'describe', 'state', 'explain', 'demonstrate understanding of ...', 'create', 'illustrate', 'quote', ' analyse' ...*) and so on.

Learning outcomes

Learning outcomes should describe what you require the pupils to do or produce by the end of the lesson, both orally and written, as well as the quantitative and qualitative aspects of their work. They should include the skills and the prior learning they will need in order to fulfil the learning outcomes. Thus: *By the end of the lesson the pupils will have produced ... (a two-side essay on ..., delivered a speech to ... about ..., discussed with ..., drawn or illustrated ..., performed ...)* and so on.

If you are covering an exam class in Years 10 or 11 you should be working alongside the HoD to plan your lessons in accordance with the scheme of work and the exam board syllabus. It is good practice to have the syllabus documents with you and use their marking criteria, detailed descriptions of various grade requirements and so on to inform your planning. These can be downloaded from the exam board websites or obtained from the exam boards themselves.

In a primary school, you will probably find yourself working with one of the team of teachers responsible for a particular year group, and much of the planning might well have been done for you. However, that should not stop you from offering contributions of your own which can be added to their schemes of work.

What to consider when planning your lesson

Effective lesson planning is more than writing down what they are going to be doing in the lesson. I've briefly mentioned learning objectives and lesson outcomes above. What else should you consider?

Social, Moral, Cultural, Spiritual (SMCS) and Every Child Matters (ECM)

These need not be incorporated into every lesson plan, but if you can see an opportunity to include them they add to the effectiveness of your lesson and to the broadening of ideas and concepts for the pupils. Try to avoid the mind-set that these are the domain of the RE or PSHE teacher. They are everyone's responsibility.

Literacy, Numeracy

As with SMCS, these will not necessarily fit every lesson plan, but should be borne in mind nevertheless. For example, as an English teacher at some stage I always teach Shakespearean sonnets by means of mathematics – 14 lines, 3 quatrains and a rhyming couplet, 10 syllables to the line and so on.

Assessment for Learning (AfL)

This is the means you employ to evaluate and assess the work done by the pupils in terms of their responses to the information and classroom tasks they have been given. Seating plans are sometimes used to good effect in AfL to help with peer assessments. Teacher questioning, pupils' contributions during the lesson, checking individual's work and plenary activities can also form part of the AfL contribution to your lesson.

Differentiation

An essential element of your lesson. However, as a supply teacher, you will need some detailed knowledge of your classes before you can start to differentiate the work effectively. Your HoD should be of assistance here, or alternatively the SEN staff will have a list of pupils with special needs including their learning requirements, strengths and weaknesses, individual education plans and so on. Bear in mind that differentiation is not the sole preserve of the weaker pupils. You might have gifted and talented pupils in your class whose work is in as much need of differentiation as that of the weaker pupils.

Resources

These should be listed in your lesson plan, and don't forget to mention any books, DVDs, websites, etc. that you have used so that the returning teacher can see the scope of the work you have done with their class. As a supply teacher in a primary or secondary school, you should have full access to the department's or school's resources, stockroom, ICT equipment, etc. It is your responsibility to take care of these resources and to return them when your assignment finishes. If you can add to them with your own home-made resources, all the better!

Homework

Include some indication of what homework tasks you want the pupils to do. Check with your HoD/team members about homework policy and timings. Ideas for homework assignments mostly arise from the lesson content, but try to avoid giving too many homework tasks that merely require the pupils to complete their classwork. Have a range of other ideas ready. Blooms Taxonomy can give you some guidance and suggestions for creating homework tasks.

Lesson content

The heart of the lesson plan! It is here that you list the teaching and learning strategies and sequences, the planned events (with approximate timings), what the pupils – and you, the teacher – will be doing during the course of the lesson, including the starter activities and plenary session.

Briefly your lesson plan in outline should look something like this:

- Introduce the new learning – lesson objectives explained and written into exercise books.
- Starter activity – related to main content or perhaps previous lesson content (if appropriate).
- New content introduced – discuss with class what they are going to be doing during your lesson – modelling, demonstrating and explaining.
- Series of tasks – main activities for pupils and teacher, with timings and periodic feedback at the end of each

activity if appropriate. You might need to use extension activities during this part of the lesson for those who have finished the main tasks. Don't forget variety, challenge and differentiation.

● Plenary – Q&A, forming conclusions, things learnt, key points, referral back to objectives to give lesson a sense of unity and completeness.

● Get class ready to leave the room – tidy up, collect resources, calm pupils ready to leave, and dismiss pupils in an orderly fashion.

Long-term assessment

If you are planning a series of lessons for a long-term assignment, you should take into account how the whole scheme (i.e. the entirety of the lessons) is to be assessed and when. This is important for the pupils, the absent staff, the department personnel and perhaps parents if your assignment overlaps with a parents' evening.

One way to think about long-term assessments is to work backwards. Start from the end point that you wish to reach with the pupils when you are planning your series of lessons and try to judge where assessments would be most appropriate and what form they will take. These might be written and oral, teacher and pupil led assessments.

Using ICT

As ICT is now a central part of most teachers' lesson planning, it is worth devoting a separate section of this chapter to it. ICT covers an increasingly large range of topics and equipment, and while not every teacher is an expert, every teacher has to build into their lesson planning some element of ICT. As with literacy and numeracy, ICT is not the sole domain of the specific department.

I am assuming here that when you start your assignment you will make yourself fully aware of the school's ICT provision, its policies and practices, and that you request a temporary log-in user name and password. In your tour of the school, pay particular attention to the IT provision, looking at whether individual classrooms are equipped with PCs or interactive whiteboards, whether the library has computers that can be used in lessons, how the booking procedure works and so on. If possible, introduce yourself to the IT technician(s) as early as possible in your stay. You will undoubtedly need their services at some time.

If you meet the HoD/deputy head during your induction and discuss schemes of work, check the ICT component of the schemes and how you might utilise them in your lesson planning.

Before getting into specifics, what is ICT and what does it comprise? It's certainly more than just computers and includes:

● interactive whiteboards;
● video and audio equipment;
● CD/DVD/Blu-ray;
● computers – laptops, tablets and desktop;
● data projectors;
● tape recorders;
● mobile phones;
● digital cameras – still and video;
● video conferencing/Skype.

When you are planning your lessons and wish to include ICT, consider its use carefully. It's worth remembering that ICT has two main strands – to support your planning and teaching, and to support the pupils' learning and enhance their own IT skills.

Your teaching can be supported by ICT in creating teaching materials, using it for assessments, and in your planning of a series of lessons over the medium and long term.

Pupils' learning can be supported by ICT in developing expertise in handling ICT, enabling clear and interesting presentation of work, aiding the self-editing process of coursework and essays, and aiding the development of research skills using the internet.

Ask yourself:

1 Is the amount of time preparing ICT input commensurate with the effect on learning outcomes?

2 Have you thought about your ability to manipulate the technology?

3 What demands does it make on the pupils?

4 How can you encourage the pupils to be fully and actively involved in ITC as opposed to becoming passive recipients?

5 Have you considered the selection and appropriateness of material to be used?

6 Will ICT form your whole lesson or can it just be used at specific points in the lesson?

ICT and the pre-planned lesson

Often the pre-planned lesson that you will be covering will require the use of some aspect of ICT, usually computers. The absent teacher will have booked a computer room for you – or will they? It's worth checking beforehand, along with the number of computers compared to the size of the class. Frequently this type of lesson consists of tasks such as 'complete the work from the last lesson', 'prepare a PowerPoint on ...' or research on a particular topic. I have always found this type of lesson to be problematic for a number of reasons:

● What do the pupils do when they have finished copying up their work from the last lesson? Is there an alternative task for them to do?

- The amount of time spent by pupils in choosing fancy fonts and graphics for the title slide of the PowerPoint presentation.

- The general lack of skill in creating PowerPoint presentations – overloaded with 'copy and paste' text and little understanding of the actual use of such a medium.

- The lack of skill in internet research methods and the inability of many pupils to select and rewrite *in their own words* the material that is required for the task.

- The temptation to visit games sites when you are not looking.

- The length of time spent choosing what music to listen to when working at a computer. Check with the school what its policy is on pupils listening to music in class.

I offer these observations as things to be aware of and ready for if you are covering such a lesson. If you are planning your own lesson, of course, you can filter out or bypass some of these points beforehand to save a lot of time and trouble later.

ICT and your own lesson planning

Because you have much more control when planning your own lessons, you can therefore do more with ICT and attempt to use the full range of equipment available to you. If you are working in a well-resourced school, lesson planning can be made a lot easier and your lessons become more creative, exciting and productive and can actively involve the pupils to a much greater degree. You could use digital camera technology to enhance the illustrative side of coursework rather than relying on Google images (if they are not barred) or clip-art. Interactive whiteboards can be useful for all manner of classroom tasks, especially starter activities or plenary sessions. The possibilities are endless.

Most pupils will have access to a computer at home or can access the internet on smart phone equipment and this can be used creatively for homework tasks. For the odd few who haven't access to the internet, allow them to do their homework in after-school homework clubs or the library. The school librarian should be able to give you full information on this.

If you are setting a research topic for homework, try to avoid the open-ended approach which will inevitably result in pupils searching endless sites and getting nowhere. I've always found it better to suggest they limit their research to two or three well-chosen sites and to be specific about what you want them to find out. You could perhaps give them a list of sites to choose from. If you don't have these to hand, the librarian will probably come up with some ideas for you. Suggest ways that the pupils could present their findings at your next lesson – printouts, handwritten notes, school-issued memory sticks and so on. Many schools these days issue free memory sticks to pupils at the beginning of the year.

Working on the principle that most teenagers know more about computers than their teachers, you have a golden opportunity to empower them in many ways. If, for example, you are on the other side of the campus covering another lesson and know you will be a few minutes late, ask one of the pupils to set up the DVD (or whatever you are using) ready for when you arrive. They will usually be only too happy to do that for you. Obviously use your discretion and judgement here in whom you choose.

Get pupils to use the interactive whiteboard for themselves and to take charge of that aspect of your lesson. You could give them responsibility for preparing the plenary session using ICT, or introducing new learning through a series of starter activities. The really skilled operators can be used to teach the less competent during your lessons, thus freeing you up for other tasks. Pupils love to show off what they can do, especially if it makes their teachers look incompetent. Embrace it and use it for your purposes and their enhanced learning opportunities.

The school library

Along with the IT technician, the school librarian should be high on your list of 'people to get to know' when you start a new assignment. School libraries, or learning resource centres as they are more commonly known these days, are a valuable, but often under-used facility in schools, particularly in the secondary sector. They have moved a long way from just being issuers of books to pupils and have now become central to the school's teaching and learning policy, resource facility and information bank.

Many school librarians have taken on a teaching role, either leading specific lessons or acting in a support role to the main teacher. How does all this affect the supply teacher?

The Chartered Institute of Library and Information Professionals (**www.clip.org.uk**) states that 'a school's teaching team is entitled to a designated library professional who:

- Understands the curriculum and pastoral needs of the teaching staff and who will support these with managed resources;
- Will collaborate with staff on curriculum planning and development and be involved in teaching;
- Will develop partnership working with other key organisations within and beyond the school.'

How does this all translate into the everyday work of the supply teacher? The librarian will be able to assist you with lesson planning, teaching and IT requirements in the following ways:

- They will most likely have been involved in departmental curriculum planning, with the HoD, deputy head and other staff, and will have a good overview of the school's curriculum requirements that can be useful to you especially if you are new to a school or working in a department that is not your specialism.

- They will provide you with resources for topic teaching through their own book, newspaper and magazine stock, as well as through inter-library loan arrangements, including IT resources.
- Support for and active work in literacy strategies through small group or class literacy sessions.
- Identification and validation of websites for topics.
- Displaying pupils' work in the library – particularly useful if you have no permanent classroom base.
- Provision of materials for SMCS and ECM.
- Teaching information literacy – the ability to locate, evaluate, analyse and synthesise relevant information.
- Running after-school clubs – homework and revision sessions.
- Providing e-learning opportunities for staff and pupils.
- Help with differentiating material for your lessons.

Can you now afford to ignore the school librarian? Besides that impressive list of qualities and skills, it's worth remembering that the school librarian probably knows more about the pupils than the average classroom teacher, and can be invaluable to you in the early days of your assignment in identifying individual pupils, their learning needs and requirements, literacy levels, interest and hobbies and so on. Librarians are a mine of information.

Departing from your lesson plan

As Robert Burns once wrote, 'The best laid plans of mice and men ...', so your best laid lesson plans can go astray at times. The reasons for this are many and varied, ranging from your own poor planning (no excuses now, though!) to situations entirely beyond your control, such as:

- fire alarms going off with the resultant evacuation of the school;
- constant interruptions from outside, or disciplinary problems inside the classroom;
- inexperienced teachers losing the thread of a lesson because they have not internalised it before teaching it;
- activities taking longer than expected, especially if you are involved in practical activities;
- technological breakdowns;
- the pupils have already done the work (the bane of most supply teachers' lives).

If you do have to change your plans, it is always better to inform the pupils of the changes and why you are deviating from the plan. Naturally, if you are not going to see the class again because you are moving on at the end of the day, make sure you leave detailed notes for the returning teacher to inform them of what you have done.

Changing your lesson plan mid-lesson can have unexpected advantages, but it is not for the faint-hearted, inexperienced or new-to-the-school supply teacher. However, the case study below is an example of how unintended advantages can come from deviating from your lesson plan.

↗ brilliant case study

I had been working with a Year 11 GCSE top set English group for some time and knew them well. I had started on a scheme of work based on the play *An Inspector Calls*, one of their set texts.

I had planned that in this particular lesson we would look at a few selected scenes and start making notes on some of the characters – their social background, values, attitudes, relationships, etc.

▶

I started by reminding the class about the setting of the play – 1912 Edwardian Britain, the year of the Titanic disaster and two years before the outbreak of World War I. As all good tradesmen will tell you (sucking in through clenched teeth) 'There's your problem, mate.' As soon as I had finished my introductory speech, hands were going up to enquire about the Titanic, the war, social class systems and so on. Most of them, of course, had seen the Leonardo di Caprio/Kate Winslet film of *Titanic* but knew little of the sub-text of social class structures. Likewise, they knew about World War I from their history lessons, but hadn't made the connection with the play. I was beginning to wish I had just given out the A4 paper and told them to get on with their notes, but it was not to be. I sensed that most of them were genuinely interested in social class structures as they asked about why people were regarded as working class or middle class and so on.

It was clear that my planned lesson was not going to happen, so I made the decision to change my plans. We spent the next 45 minutes discussing the ins and outs of social class and applying it to the play, the Titanic and World War I. They were unaware of the way passengers aboard the Titanic were accommodated, with hoi poloi in steerage in the bowels of the ship, while the upper crust luxuriated in their private cabins at deck level. The ship thus became a metaphor for the class system in Edwardian England.

They knew about various battles in World War I, but didn't have any appreciation of how the war began the breakdown of the barriers between the social classes, with women doing men's work and the working class lads rubbing shoulders with the aristocracy amid the muck and bullets of the trenches.

At the end of the lesson, several pupils said it was the best lesson they'd had, and subsequently I knew it had been worthwhile judging from their responses to the original lesson plan at the end of their next lesson, and the essays they produced at later stages.

brilliant tip

If you are going to change plans, make sure of your ground beforehand and avoid substituting a lesson that is irrelevant or one that simply becomes an easy way out of a difficult situation, whether of your making or not.

Whatever the reason, you might find it necessary to depart from your lovingly prepared lesson plan to do something entirely unexpected and unplanned for. When you are at the early stages of your teaching career, or, in the case of a supply teacher new to a school, it is not to be recommended that you deviate from lesson plans. You should be planning very tight lessons and keeping to them as far as possible.

brilliant recap

- Lesson planning is at the heart of what we do as teachers. Your success as a supply teacher will depend to a large extent on your ability to plan effectively.
- Do not assume that all pre-planned lessons have been properly planned.
- Have a stock of emergency, one-off lesson ideas to hand. You will need them.
- Use ICT to enhance the pupils' learning and to aid your teaching, planning and assessments.
- The school library is one of the most valuable resources you have at hand to help your planning and to inform your teaching.

CHAPTER 6

Make friends with the internet

Where would we be without it? It's revolutionised our lives, our work and leisure in more ways than we can know. As a teacher I find myself using it constantly to search for information, to research topics, to prepare lessons, to construct PowerPoint presentations and a thousand and one other uses.

It's already been said that, along with a copious supply of head-ache pills, a supply teacher needs to have a bundle of lesson ideas in their stock of 'goodies' that they haul around from job to job. You just never know when you're going to need them. I would never leave home to go on a short-term assignment without checking that I had at least a few instant lesson ideas with me. The problem is they take up a lot of space and how do you know if they are suitable?

There's only so much you carry with you, so inevitably you rely on the internet and your trusty little memory stick to get you out of a fix or to supply you with the notes, information, worksheets, interactive material and so on that give you the confidence to go into a classroom knowing you are as well equipped as possible to teach your lesson. You can spend invaluable hours searching for material that will be suitable for the classes you are about to teach, especially if you are a newcomer to the job or have been 'out of the loop' for a while.

This chapter is intended to do some of the donkey work for you by looking at a range of internet sites that you might find useful.

Some of them are subject specific, while others cover a number of different subjects across the phases and Key Stages. I have tried to include sites that are suitable for primary and secondary schools and have listed the Key Stages for each site.

brilliant tip

Some sites require a subscription before you can access them. Many schools (or individual departments in the secondary sector) will already have taken out a subscription to some of the more popular sites. It's worth checking first so you don't end up spending your own money.

Note: The information contained in the websites that have been reviewed was accurate at Autumn 2011. However, as most websites are regularly updated, some information might change or be amended, or in some cases the website might no longer exist.

Subject-specific websites

English

Address

www.english-teaching.co.uk

Key Stages

Secondary (KS3 and 4)

General comments

This site, also known as FRETWEB, has a range of English resources that are now available on the TES site below. These cover the secondary age range and include general resources, lesson plans and schemes of work.

Good stuff

Some of the topics listed on the site are:

- GCSE Spoken Language Study material;
- AQA poetry anthology 'Character and Voice' cluster in Word or pdf format;
- 'Of Mice and Men' resources;
- 'An Inspector Calls' controlled assessments and examination material;
- WJEC Literature – Unseen Poetry.

All have clear links to the TES site.

All 7500 resources are free through the TES site.

Address

www.teachit.co.uk

Key Stages

Primary and secondary sectors (KS1–5)

General comments

A very comprehensive site covering all phases of education. The primary site, TeachitPrimary, is separate from the secondary one and requires separate registration. Although there are a lot of free resources on Teachit, which you can access after registering, much of the material is only available by subscription. The rates, as of April 2011, are as follows:

- Teachit.plus – individual or department £49.95;
- Teachit.works – individual £99.95;
- Teachit.works – department £495.

The 'Join Us' link will give you full details.

Good stuff

Visit the 'Whizzy things' area in the primary and secondary areas for some 'super powerful and wonderfully flexible' fun ideas. However, most of them are only available for subscribers.

The 'Staffroom' section is a forum for teachers to express their views, get advice or just get something off their chest on a range of subjects.

Lots of literacy and numeracy resources and interactive whiteboard activities in the primary area.

Click on 'Resource libraries' for media studies and drama material for KS4.

Easy site to navigate, with clear links to partner sites.

Click on 'Resource libraries' for 'Teaching tools' – a collection of teaching and admin. suggestions for planning, teaching, marking, assessments, etc.

The 'Bookshop' section contains a number of books and DVDs that are available through the site. One in particular, 'Take Cover', contains 36 stand-alone KS3 photocopiable lessons, four project-based lessons for long-term cover, a selection of one-off lessons from the Teachit site, instructions and worksheets for the cover teacher or the teacher setting cover lessons. However, at £99.00 plus £5.50 p&p, for non-members, it might prove a bit expensive!

Address
www.teachingenglish.org.uk

Key Stages
KS1–4
Primary, secondary and tertiary

General comments

A very comprehensive site, run by the British Council and the BBC, covering areas not usually found on other English subject sites. Topics covered include:

- teaching resources (activities, lesson plans, BritLit, videos of teachers giving tips);
- teacher development (CPD, books, conferences, etc.);
- training courses (British Council on-line courses, downloadable worksheets, teaching speaking);
- articles (on many aspects of language teaching);
- community (forum, polls, blogs, video material).

A particularly useful site if you are teaching pupils for whom English is not their first language, but materials can be used equally well with other pupils.

Registration is free and allows you to download materials, be in contact with English teachers across the world and have access to new materials as soon as they become available.

Good stuff

Click on 'Teaching resources' and then 'Lesson plans' tab to lead you to an A to Z of contents. Saves a lot of fruitless searching for lesson ideas.

Each lesson plan includes the topic, age range, level of ability, timing and objectives.

BritLit section has a range of free downloadable resources for teaching literature to primary, secondary and adult age ranges.

Each page has a full directory to help you navigate around the site, with links to partner sites as well.

After registering, you can keep up-to-date with new materials and discussions via Twitter, Facebook or through the site's newsletter.

Maths

Address

www.mymaths.co.uk

Key Stages

KS1–5

(Primary, secondary, Post-16 and special schools)

General comments

MyMaths is a subscription website which offers a 'fully inter-active, on-line mathematical solution for all ages and abilities' and is used in over 70 countries by 4 million pupils. If you are teaching maths as a supply teacher, check with your school if it has a subscription to MyMaths. Subscription rates are high, ranging from £210 + VAT for primary schools to £450 + VAT for secondary schools.

Areas covered are lessons, homework, booster material, assessment, games, Post-16 maths, GCSE Stats.

Good stuff

Promotes independent learning.

Parents can be involved with on-line homework tasks.

Hundreds of ready-made lessons covering all Key Stages.

Excellent resources and easy-to-use site for non-specialist teachers, such as supply staff.

Well-established site with thousands of users.

Address

www.mathszone.co.uk

Key Stages

KS1–4

General comments

In its own words: 'This site aims to bring collect together and order a range of free resources discovered on the Internet, which can be used for teaching maths in Primary Schools in the UK.' It covers the secondary sector as well, but with fewer resources!

Click on 'Key Objs' on the homepage for a list of interactive resources from a variety of sites covering Year 1 to Year 6.

The KS1/KS2 tab takes you to a wide variety of maths resources, including fractions, decimals, percentages, ratios, place values, estimating and so on.

The KS3/KS4 tab takes you to resources on multiplication, division, addition, subtraction, algebra, shape and space, and data handling.

Good stuff

A lot of primary maths material.

Easy navigation.

Collects resources from a variety of other sites.

Address

www.mathsisfun.com

Key Stages

Approximate age range 5/6 to 17/18

General comments

An American site with resources from K (Kindergarten) to Grade 12 (Year 13 Post-16). Topics covered include data, geometry, puzzles, numbers, algebra, money (in a variety of national currencies), measurement and games.

Good stuff

Clear, colourful site with easy navigation.

Site updated on a regular basis.

Pupil friendly.

Illustrated maths dictionary.

Printable or on-line worksheets, with answer facility.

Address

http://uk.ixl.com

Key Stages

Reception to KS3 (Year 9)

General comments

A comprehensive interactive site covering early years up to Year 9 in KS3.

Most year groups have over 200 activities listed, apart from the Reception year which has 41.

At the bottom of the homepage there are links to the National Curricula of England, Scotland, Wales and Northern Ireland that outline the curriculum content for each Key Stage, including the Knowledge, Skills and Understanding and Breadth of Knowledge.

Good stuff

For each activity, hover the cursor over the task to see a sample problem or click on the activity for the real thing.

Each activity has a countdown clock and scoreboard.

An easy site to navigate with clear indications of year groups and topics.

Science

Address

www.schoolscience.co.uk

Key Stages

1–5

General comments

A very comprehensive site with over 700 resources that covers all age ranges up to 19, and is brought to you by the Association for Science Education.

Click on the age range required on left hand side of homepage, then click 'view resources' and follow the instructions on the top of each page.

Good stuff

Easy to navigate with clear instructions.

Has sections that offer 'Giveaways' (free material for teachers), competitions and events.

ScienceLink takes you to a long list of science websites that cover a multitude of science topics – biology, chemistry, physics, earth sciences, science careers, etc.

Teacher Zone is worth looking at as well. Lots of resources for teachers – CPD, courses and exams, discovery centres and museums and so on.

Address

www.canalmuseum.org.uk

On the homepage, click on Home and then Education. This takes you to Teacher zone, Learning zone and Parent zone.

The Teacher zone has a drop-down menu from the National

Curriculum tab for each key stage with lesson plans, activities and teachers' notes.

Key Stages
KS1–3

General comments
A single subject site but with many topics from the London Canal Museum about the history of canals, canal wildlife, locks, bridges, tunnels and the future of canals. Contains a number of lesson plans, with learning objectives, differentiation, resources and materials sheet.

The Learning zone has a number of interesting and clear interactive tasks for pupils.

Particularly useful either as pre-visit preparation or post-visit activities in the classroom, but can equally well be used as stand-alone material.

Good stuff
Simple, clear, downloadable and interactive material. A number of KS2 activities are in pdf format.

Clear links to National Curriculum requirements, particularly in history and geography, but also maths and art.

An unusual and fascinating topic for all ages.

General sites

The following sites contain materials for most National Curriculum subjects in the primary and secondary sectors.

Address
www.tes.co.uk

Key Stages
Foundation, primary (KS1 and 2), secondary (KS3, 4, 5), whole school and special needs.

General comments
An incredibly useful site for all things to do with teaching. It covers jobs, teaching community issues (with a range of different forums for you to air your views on many education-related topics), teaching resources, careers advice, etc.

Has excellent resources for all subjects within your chosen Key Stage, which include lesson plans, activities, games, teaching ideas and worksheets. It is constantly updated and if you register it will send you regular emails with the latest resources, many of them targeted at specific events or times of the year, such as Christmas teaching suggestions, or national events such as the Royal Wedding in 2011. It claims to have over 63,000 free teaching resources.

Good stuff
You can upload, adapt, edit and download classroom activities.

Good, clear links to partner websites, including the *Times Educational Supplement* newspaper.

Regular email updates full of excellent classroom activities, lesson plans and so on if you register with the site.

An easy site to navigate.

Address
www.teachingideas.co.uk

Key Stages
KS1–4, but mainly primary. Secondary activities are labelled '11+'

General comments

A very comprehensive site with hundreds of activities, resources, ideas across all the core subjects (literacy, maths, science), as well as ICT, DT, PE, Art, Music, PSHE, Early Years and so on. Hover the cursor over the subject that you want and a drop-down menu gives you the main topics within the subject. This will then take you to the lessons plans and materials that are downloadable as pdf, Word or PowerPoint files. Others are interactive resources. Each activity is labelled according to the age range for which it is suitable.

The homepage contains areas for a featured topic, latest news, sharing ideas with other teachers, mailing list to get up-to-date information and news, and links to Facebook and Twitter.

Good stuff

Easy to navigate, with lots of colourful and easy to read information.

Click on the 'More' heading at the top of the homepage and it takes you to a number of activities and resources for lesson planning, assessment, special needs and assemblies.

The 'Themes' tab links you to a number of theme-based resources suitable for all Key Stage years.

Some activities are labelled 'Purple Mash'. If you're not already familiar with them, 'Purple Mash' apps (or 'app-tivities') from 2Simple are interactive tools that children can use in a wide range of curriculum areas. They are all free to use and are a wonderful resource for teachers to use as part of their lessons.' Go to **www.teemeducation.org.uk** for more information about Purple Mash. On the homepage of this site click on 'Primary' and in drop-down menu, click on 'Creative and other tools'. Purple Mash appears in that drop-down menu.

Address

www.bbc.co.uk/schools/bitesize

Key Stages

KS1–4, Bitesize TGAU (Welsh), Scottish Standard Grade and Highers

General comments

Possibly the most comprehensive site of them all, covering a huge range of subjects, topics and age ranges. The English National Curriculum section comprises:

- KS1 – maths and literacy;
- KS2 – English, maths and science;
- KS3 – English, maths and science;
- KS4 GCSE – all GCSE subjects.

The Welsh and Scottish sections have their own subjects and topics.

Most of the resources are interactive and very user friendly, with clear instructions. Topics and subjects are easy to find and have a 'revise, test' format for pupils to use. Some have video links as well.

Being a BBC site, you have links to other BBC on-line facilities, such as news, weather, sport, iPlayer, TV and radio and so on.

Navigation is very easy and clear to take you to interactive material.

Go into any of the Key Stage areas and click on the 'BBC Teachers' link for a range of resources and activities, lesson plans and worksheets for all age ranges.

Good stuff

Almost too many to list, but a few stand out.

The video clips in the interactive material are very good, with key points listed to aid pupils' understanding.

Message boards for pupils to talk to each other about various subjects that they are studying and their concerns about them.

The 'Teachers' site is very useful, not only for lesson plans and materials, but for general information for teachers, news, comments, competitions and links to other sites which you might find useful.

Class clips on the 'Teachers' page lists more than 7,500 video clips from BBC programmes that can be used in the classroom. Simply enter a subject or topic in the search box and press 'Go'.

A new section is News for Schools with links to BBC Newsround topics, news about the latest developments in a range of school subjects and the latest world news podcasts, all of which you can use in the classroom.

Address
www.woodlands-junior.kent.sch.uk

Key Stages
KS1–2

General comments
A website developed and run by Woodlands Junior School, Kent that contains a remarkably wide range of interactive and other resources for pupils and teachers.

As well as school information, the main curriculum areas covered are:

- Maths Zone
- Literacy Zone
- Science
- Homework Help

- Geography
- History

and a range of other interesting and useful information sections, including London, Festivals & Celebrations, The British Royal Family, London 2012, Day, Night & the Seasons and so on. Within each area there are interactive tasks, lots of information, question and answer sections and links to other websites.

Good stuff
Attractively designed homepage.

Easy navigation around the site.

Regularly updated.

Clear links to other useful websites.

Guest Book where you can leave your comments on the site. It's worth reading some of the very positive comments from teachers and pupils from all over the country.

Address
www.primaryresources.co.uk

Key Stages
Early Years, KS1–2 with some KS3 material

General comments
A comprehensive site covering all the subjects at KS1 and 2, and including classroom management aids, pupil aids and target sheets, assembly ideas and multinational special days and celebrations.

Navigation is quick and easy and takes you to a multitude of resources in different formats – Word docs, pdf files, PowerPoint. Most activities are interactive, but there are downloadable and printable resources as well.

Good stuff

The other 'Primary' links are worth looking at – Primary Extra, Primary Interactive.co.uk, Primary Resources, Primary Displays and Primary Forums.

Activities, lesson ideas and worksheets are clearly labelled with age range and key stage symbols. These are found on the left-hand side of the homepage. Click on the 'symbol indicator' at the bottom of any subject page for a full explanation of the symbols used. There's a useful comparative chart that gives you the equivalent year groupings of pupils in other countries.

Clear links to other websites.

Teacher Forum facility to swap ideas and make general comments.

Address

www.channel4learning.com

Key Stages

KS1–4 with Scottish equivalent levels

General comments

'The home of online education resources, games and activities for primary and secondary schools' run by Channel 4.

The navigation panel on the left-hand side of the homepage allows you to toggle between primary and secondary subject resources. Click on your chosen subject and it takes you to a resource filter so that you can specify what years, key stage(s), subject and topic you wish to search for.

Many of the resources on this site are linked to Channel 4 programmes and the site supplies you with teacher programme notes that include Aims, Outlines of the programme, Curriculum Relevance, Background, Activities and Links to other relevant websites.

Interactive resources are easy to navigate and colourful in their presentation and can be used by teachers or pupils in the classroom or at home.

Good stuff

The homepage links to:

- on-line shop with books, CD-ROMs and DVDs; downloadable primary and secondary brochures in pdf format;
- gcsEASE digital learning resources in engineering, applied science, applied business, leisure and tourism, health and social care and applied ICT for teachers and pupils;
- Clipbank with more than 800 hours of award-winning programmes. Click on 'Learn More' tab at top of the Clipbank homepage for full details of what it can offer.

Address

www.bbc.co.uk/skillswise

Key Stages

Not specified on the site, but appropriate for KS2, 3, lower ability KS4 and adults wishing to improve English and Maths skills.

General comments

Another very useful and comprehensive site from the BBC.

It contains a huge amount of material for 'Word' and 'Number' work, with interactive areas and downloadable worksheets (with answer sheets as well), quizzes, games and factsheets for each topic covered.

The 'Word' section covers grammar, spelling, reading, writing, listening and vocabulary.

The 'Number' section covers whole numbers; measures, shapes and space; fractions, decimals, percentages; and data handling.

Click on 'Skillswise materials A–Z' on the homepage for a full alphabetical list of everything on the site.

Good stuff

Attractive site that is easy to navigate.

Downloadable Skillswise CD-ROM facility.

Quick Reads section on homepage lists a number of 'bite-sized books by bestselling writers and celebrities'. Each book has an on-screen 'taster' extract, and audio file and a downloadable pdf version of Chapter 1.

Interactive 'Games' section located on the homepage is ideal for starter activities in 'Word' and 'Number'. Games are timed and pupils can choose different levels according to speed and ability.

Other useful sites

- **www.sitesforteachers.com** An American site with pages of links to other websites on a wide range of subjects and years groups.

- **www.chalkface.com** This site features a wide range of resources for secondary pupils and teachers. There is some free material, but others are for sale in book, CD-ROM or downloadable forms.

- **www.engagingplaces.org.uk** A website that contains lesson plans and teaching resources about architecture and design and great places to visit or learn about. Covers main key stages and contains 629 resources, 516 venues and 378 articles.

- **www.schoolzone.co.uk** Schoolzone web guide provides links to over 60,000 web-based resources across all key stages. Searchable by keywords, subject and age range.

 **recap**

- The list of websites provided here is by no means an exhaustive one. However, they are some of the more useful, comprehensive and easy to use sites that I and other teachers have come across.

- All the websites listed have resources that are interactive or downloadable in electronic or paper form for use in the classroom or as homework tasks.

- A number of sites contain forums that cover many areas of concern for teachers. The TES forum has a specific area for supply teachers.

- The information contained in each website entry was accurate at the time of writing, but as most of the websites mentioned are updated fairly regularly, some aspects might change over time.

- Many of the sites allow you to upload your own material, or to edit and amend the downloadable materials.

CHAPTER 7

Survival in the classroom

magine having a job in which you start afresh every day, in a different place with different people, never establishing yourself or settling into an environment that you can call your own. Would you do that willingly? Yes, if you are a supply teacher going from one school to another on a daily basis.

Even if you secure a week's work at a school you might still feel that your job has no sense of permanency and that as soon as you have started, the end of the week has arrived and off you go to start somewhere else on Monday.

This type of transient work routine can lead to frustration and a sense of disappointment in one's own abilities and thus to a diminution of one's skills so carefully honed over the years. In turn that can lead to complacency and indifference. If you are new to supply teaching, it might seem quite exciting at first moving from one place to another, but, like rock bands on tour, it can soon lose its appeal if you go from one bad experience to another.

Is it actually worth going through the hassle of following up on a breach of discipline if tomorrow you are going to be in a different school? Why should a supply teacher bother to create the right atmosphere in a classroom if it's only going to last a day or two? Is it worth getting to know anyone in the school when you might never see them again?

These questions are difficult to answer, and at the end of a long and arduous day it is so much easier to pack your bag, walk away and ignore the fact that some little Year 9 charmer has just lobbed a chair at you. However, difficult though it may be, at some stage in your supply teaching career you will have to face these questions and find your own solutions.

As a professional you have a responsibility, no matter how long or short a time you are in the school, to act in accordance with the rules and standards of the school and with your own personal and professional standards. Put yourself in the position of the absent teacher returning the next day. Would you want to come back to your class to find all hell had broken loose and that nothing had been done about it? As a supply teacher you are acting in place of the regular teacher and you have the same responsibilities for what happens in your classroom. But while you are there, the classroom is *your* classroom. You are in charge, not the pupils! And, of course, you never know, you might go back there and be faced with the same pupils. Where will your professional credibility be then?

Creating the right atmosphere, employing all your classroom management skills and showing the pupils you mean business when it comes to disciplinary matters can only do you good in the long term, even if it seems pointless at the time.

Not being in control of the physical environment in which you are working can be frustrating and annoying too, but remember you are to some extent a guest in that classroom and you should respect that fact even if it means working in a tip for a day or two. If you are there for a long-term assignment then you can establish some order and tidiness so that you can do the job to the best of your ability. Strangely enough, pupils don't like untidy rooms either!

If you are in the same room for all your lessons over a long period, which can apply to both primary and secondary supply work, it becomes your responsibility to ensure that the physical space is looked after and any problems are reported to the appropriate person, including your immediate line manager (HoD or similar) and possibly the caretaker. This becomes especially important if the problem becomes, or has the potential to be, a health and safety risk. Such items as:

- frayed carpets or floor tiles;
- broken or damaged chairs;
- broken windows;
- electrical faults;
- leaks from radiators or through windows and ceilings;
- faulty door and cupboard locks;
- blinds, curtains and blackouts that are faulty or damaged, should all be reported.

brilliant tip

Your management of the physical environment and of the people in it is the key to your survival in the classroom as a supply teacher.

So, what is this elusive thing called 'classroom management'?

Well, it comprises a wide and varied range of strategies and tactics, most of which can be taught, but some will be more instinctive and will represent aspects of you as a person. It's not all about behaviour either. Management in the classroom is about:

- Time management – making sure the lesson doesn't over or under run; being aware of the structure of the lesson and the timings of each section.
- People management – the pupils and any other adults such as teaching assistants.
- Resource management – the pupils' books and folders, IT equipment, resources belonging to the department, school or absent teacher.

- Physical space management – where pupils sit, arrangement of desks, the use of furniture (such as chairs, bookcases and cupboards), how pupils move around the room, arrangements for small group work.

Let's start at the beginning.

Entering the classroom

Whether you are in a primary or secondary school, control of the classroom environment can make or break a lesson. Gaining control of it from the start is important so, where possible, be there before the pupils. This way you are in control and have a psychological advantage which can determine in part how the lesson proceeds from that point.

Exude confidence and welcome the pupils with a smile and a 'hello'. Ask them to sit in their normal seats and ensure all the formalities – taking off outdoor coats, getting books and equipment out of bags and so on – are done quickly, quietly and efficiently. If your HoD, deputy head, or subject leader has done their job properly, you should have a seating plan and register for each class. Check that they are up-to-date.

Many secondary schools expect each lesson to begin with the taking of a register. It is good practice anyway even if the school does not work that way. It allows you to keep control at the beginning of proceedings by requesting silence when calling the register and it sets the right business-like tone for the lesson. At the same time you can check with your seating plan if everyone is in the right place. This procedure is less relevant in many primary schools as you are likely to be with the same group of pupils throughout the day.

Learn to 'read the class' as they enter. There are many tell-tale signs to look for. Observe how the class approaches the room. Do they automatically line up outside before being asked to enter? Is there excessive noise and movement, or do they approach quietly and with a sense of discipline? Do they look smart and appear ready to work? Once they are in, do they get out books and other materials without being asked, or just sit there waiting to be told?

If they come in to your room in an orderly fashion, acknowledge your presence and even respond to your greeting, then the chances are you will have much less of a problem than with the class that noisily barges past you and doesn't even know you're there. If they do enter that way, do something about it!

brilliant tip

At the very least remind pupils about good manners and courtesy. If necessary, have them line up outside the room and require them to enter properly. Remind them of the school's policy about politeness and courtesy. All schools have one even if you don't know chapter and verse of it!

Perhaps the above points are more relevant to the secondary sector where pupils move from lesson to lesson much more than primary pupils would do. However, if you are in a primary school, your presence in the classroom should be acknowledged in the same way as it would be in a secondary school, and you should observe behaviour and attitude at the start of a lesson in the same way.

There will be times when your lateness is unavoidable, particularly in a big school where you might have a distance to travel between lessons. If your assignment requires you to be in a different classroom for each lesson and you have to walk half way across the campus each time, then you can be forgiven if you are a few minutes late. If you know in advance that this might happen, you could ask another member of the department just to keep an eye on the class until you get there. If that isn't possible, you need to assert control as soon as possible. In a primary school your lateness to a lesson is less likely as you will be with the same class for most of the day anyway.

I always make it a practice to apologise for my lateness and explain what happened. Pupils, by and large, are a fairly forgiving bunch. Equally, you should expect pupils who are late to apologise and to explain themselves as well. If the lateness is genuine – another member of staff wanted to see the pupil or they were late leaving the previous class, for example – ask if the pupil has a note from the teacher. This is the policy in many schools, though not strictly adhered to, I fear.

The most important thing here is to get the lesson underway as soon as possible in an orderly, professional manner. If you are suspicious of the excuse given by a pupil, leave any further action until later, perhaps at the end of the lesson or some convenient time during the lesson, when you can pursue the matter to your satisfaction.

It's always worth 'setting out your stall' at the beginning of the lesson with information about how you expect the class to behave and some basic ground rules of good behaviour and courtesy. At this stage of their lesson, all they know is that you are a stranger in their environment. They know nothing about you or what you are like as a person or a teacher. They will be somewhat suspicious of you at first and might be resentful of your presence, particularly if they have had a succession of supply teachers over the past few lessons. Showing that you mean business (that is, that you are professional, competent, well organised and so on) and know how to handle a class will stand you in good stead.

Knowing the school's rules on behaviour and its code of conduct will help you, of course, to set the right tone from the start, but if it's your first day and you haven't had time to absorb all the information given to you in your induction, then rely on your own good sense and experience. Most of what you will tell them will adhere to the school's rules anyway.

Although it can be a daunting prospect being in front of a strange group of pupils for the first time, avoid showing nervousness and fear. They will sense it and will often exploit it!

Introduce yourself and write your name on the board. Be prepared for the 'Are you a real teacher?' question and 'When is Mr X coming back?' Answer them honestly and politely. Some teachers who are new to the job can feel that pupils are being rude and impolite by asking these questions. Mostly they are not. They are simply adjusting themselves to their new circumstances and checking you out.

brilliant tip

Young people, on the whole, don't like change. It disturbs them and unsettles their routine. Be aware of that and be sensitive towards it.

If time permits, it's worth putting the lesson information on the board before the start of the lesson and having the books or equipment ready to go. Generally speaking you probably won't have such a luxury and you therefore have to get started as soon as possible. Write the lesson objectives on the board and ask the pupils to write these into their books. This gives you breathing space to organise your thoughts and read through the lesson notes one more time. Ask a pupil to hand out the exercise books. It saves time and of course they know everyone and you don't.

Learn to summarise information and adopt a 'shorthand' method – using abbreviations, shortened versions of words, symbols, figures instead of words – to save writing screeds of notes on the board while World War III is breaking out behind you. Talk through the lesson plan with them first – you can always put extra notes on the board when the lesson is under way. Make sure that what you've said to them makes sense and they understand what's required. A good way to assess this is to ask pupils to repeat the essentials of the instructions you have just given them. This can be done as a Q&A session around the class as part of a starter activity.

If the lesson has been set for you, follow the plan as outlined. Assume the absent teacher has set the order and content of the lesson deliberately, not just as a fill-in. With luck your lesson plan will include starter and plenary activities. If not, it's worth having a few tricks up your sleeve to get the attention and interest of the pupils (dealt with in Chapter 5 on lesson planning).

And so your lesson is under way!

The pupils are quiet, diligent, getting on with their lesson with enthusiasm and interest. You could hear a pin drop. Then you wake from your dream and realise that it's not really like that at all. Pupils are shouting out that they don't know what to do, they're bored, asking how long it is to break time, demanding to go to the toilet and so on.

In response it's no use shouting, 'I've already told you that' or 'It's not my fault you weren't listening.' You have to deal with each pupil at a time and keep from losing the control you fought so hard for at the start. Politely ask them to put up their hands if they have a question or something to say to you and tell them to wait until you can get to them.

brilliant tip

Try to position yourself so that if you are talking to one pupil, you can keep an eye on the rest of the class as well. Develop the 'third eye' – in the back of the head is a good place! Keep monitoring the class for those needing help or those getting restless. Never sit down for any length of time. A seated teacher is an invisible teacher to the class. Even if you have an exceptional class that is working hard and appears not to need your intervention, it is good practice to wander round, asking occasionally if everything is all right and if they understand the work. Not every pupil likes asking for help in front of their classmates, especially from a stranger.

Practise the art of listening to one pupil and being able to hear and monitor what's going on around you at the same time. If you can do that successfully, it's a great psychological weapon in your armoury and shows the pupils that you are in control. Always clamp down on behaviour that you consider unacceptable and that you know would not be tolerated in normal circumstances.

Of the four aspects of classroom management, the hardest and, in some cases, the most feared, is people management which usually translates to behaviour management.

It's difficult enough for experienced, full-time teachers to deal with bad behaviour at times, so supply teachers might have an even more daunting prospect when they are new to a school and a particular class. If you ask at your induction what such and such a class is like, you will rarely be told the brutal truth if they are bad. It will be couched in the 'well, some of the pupils can be a little challenging at times, but I'm sure you'll cope' type of language. And we all know what that means!

Like any other teacher you'll be faced with a range of problems in the classroom, but being a supply teacher will mean that you are to some extent at a disadvantage to start with. They say that knowledge is power, but at this stage you will not necessarily have the knowledge that will help you to overcome some of the problems. Recently I was teaching a small group and became irritated by one pupil who refused point blank to read out something he'd written in the lesson and would only answer me in monosyllabic mumblings. When I spoke to another member of staff about him, I discovered he had a severe stammer and was getting help from a speech therapist. One of the things that exacerbated his stammer was talking to strangers. His reluctance to communicate was thus explained and from that point onwards we got on well as I made allowances for his speech impediment.

What might you face in the classroom that comes under the heading of behaviour management?

Conflict in the classroom

No matter how good a school you are in, there will always be some form of conflict to deal with. It might be the very low level 'Sir, he's nicked my pen.' 'No I haven't, you liar,' variety to the high tariff, all-out fight between pupils.

If you are faced with the latter and you feel that you can't – or don't want to – cope with it, then you have no choice but to send for help. In a secondary school, the head of department should be your first port of call. Send a pupil to find the person you need. In a primary school it's more likely to be the deputy head who would deal with this sort of situation. If you have a TA in the class with you, use them to summon help or to assist you in defusing the situation.

In extreme circumstances, be careful to avoid physical contact with pupils; ensure that you and others are out of harm's way and that the protagonists will not injure themselves on chairs or table edges. Send for help immediately. These events are, fortunately, very rare, but they do happen and you need to know what to do!

However, the school expects you to be able to deal with most disciplinary matters yourself and you should aim to do so. A number of incidents in the classroom can be attributed to poor planning by the teacher and therefore you need to be conscious of this when you are planning your lessons. Poor lesson planning leads to boredom and irritability by pupils, which can in turn cause conflict between you and them.

If you see, for example, that the work set by the absent teacher is not enough for the length of lesson, then you need to do something about it before the lesson. If you have time, see the head of department and ask if they think the lesson content is suitable and could they suggest some supplementary work. In a primary school it would be worth asking another member of the team to look at the lesson plan with you and decide if it is appropriate.

If you have set the work yourself, run it past the head of department first if you are not sure about its viability either in terms of length or suitability for the class's ability range.

Pupils' behavioural problems are a constant in most schools and can be the area that challenges the supply teacher most. If you are in the school for a long assignment, you will get to know your classes and the 'characters' to watch. After a few days you will become accepted and you will be able to deal with the problems more effectively. However, if you are in for just a day or two you will need to adopt a different approach to bad behaviour.

A recent study into pupil behaviour *Managing Pupil Behaviour – Key Issues in Teaching and Learning* (Routledge, 2006) undertaken by Terry Haydn of the University of East Anglia showed up some interesting points on how teachers feel about pupil discipline and how they cope with it. According to the survey, Ofsted stated that discipline was inadequate in *less than 1% of schools* while at the same time 17,000 pupils were excluded for poor behaviour in the year of the study. I suspect that most teachers would find that 1% figure laughable and most of us at some time in our careers have faced serious breaches of discipline in the classroom or in the corridors and play areas.

Haydn developed a 10-point scale to describe the sorts of behaviour that teachers face and asked them how they fared. I have reproduced the scale below. Bearing in mind that the majority of teachers who responded would be full-time members of staff, it might be useful to consider it from a supply teacher's point of view with the added problems of being new to a school and to the classes you are covering. I know many supply teachers who might feel that they perpetually operate in the 6–5 or below categories, but even experienced teachers will find themselves in those areas as well from time to time.

Because the experienced, full-time teacher will have much better knowledge about the classes than will the supply teacher, they should be able to cope with the discipline problems more effectively in the majority of cases. However, if you are on a long-term supply assignment, you will also have to deal with discipline problems in the same way. Knowing where you are on the scale is one thing; how to cope with it is quite another.

brilliant activity

How well do you fare on the scale? (Haydn's 10-point scale)

10 You feel completely relaxed, able to undertake any form of lesson activity without concern. You and the pupils work together, enjoying the experience.

9 You feel completely in control and can undertake any sort of activity, but you need to exercise authority at times, in a friendly way, to maintain a calm, purposeful working atmosphere.

8 You can maintain a relaxed and co-operative working atmosphere, but this requires thought and effort at times. Some forms of lesson activity may be under less control than others.

7 You can maintain a co-operative working atmosphere and undertake any form of classroom activity, but this requires more considerable thought and effort.

6   It is often a major effort to establish and maintain a relaxed, calm
    atmosphere. Several pupils will not remain on task without persistent
    surveillance, exhortation or threats. It is sometimes difficult to
    get pupils to be quiet while you are talking, but there is no major
    disruption.

5   Your control is limited, and there are times when you would be
    embarrassed if the head walked in. The atmosphere is rather chaotic
    at times, with several pupils manifestly not listening to you. But
    pupils who want to work can get on with it, albeit in a rather noisy
    atmosphere.

4   Your control is limited: it takes time and effort to get the class to listen.
    You try to get onto the worksheet or written part of the lesson fairly
    quickly in order to get their heads down. Pupils talk while you are
    talking, and minor transgressions go unpunished because too many
    occur. You try to keep a lid on things and concentrate on those pupils
    who are trying to work.

3   There is major disruption and many pupils pay little attention to your
    presence. Swearwords may go unchecked and pupils walk round the
    room at will. When you write on the board, objects are thrown around
    the room.

2   The pupils largely determine what goes on. You take materials into the
    lesson, but once distributed they are ignored, drawn on or made into
    paper aeroplanes. When you write on the board, objects are thrown at
    you rather than around the room.

1   Your entry into the classroom is greeted by jeers and abuse. There are
    so many transgressions of the rules it is difficult to know where to start.
    You wish you had not gone into teaching.

Source: 'How good is discipline in schools today?', TES website, ww.tes.co.uk

Whether we like it or not, pupil behaviour and attitudes towards
teachers have changed over the years. It is no longer a given that
Year 7 pupils, for example, are polite and malleable and will do
everything you tell them without demur. Even at the tender age

of 11, they know – or think they know – their rights and are often not afraid to voice them. We've all come across pupils who act like barrack room lawyers from time to time and assert their presence in a loud and aggressive manner.

Unfortunately our presence and booming voices cut little ice with those sorts of pupils and, in fact, only make matters worse. You need to use your intelligence, pupil interaction skills, knowledge of the school policies and code of conduct and employ your sense of humour (if you still have one) to deal with the loud mouth, verbally aggressive pupil.

One thing to avoid in the middle of a lesson is a slanging match with these pupils. Such pupils will probably have displayed poor behaviour from the start of the lesson. They will be talking to their friends when you are trying to start the lesson; little work will have been achieved; an angry and rebellious attitude will have been displayed. Keep calm and act professionally at all times.

If an argument should arise, it is always good practice to remove the pupil from the 'audience' – their classmates. Ask the pupil to step out into the corridor where you can deal with the situation more calmly and out of the public gaze. You could try inviting the pupil to discuss their supposed grievances with the head at the end of the day. I find this usually calms things down.

The working atmosphere in a classroom has a big influence on pupil attainment and you will find that for most of the time most pupils acknowledge that they are there to work, and not to mess around. A good working atmosphere is vital if your lesson is to achieve its intended outcomes, but you have to work at it. You might not always achieve the level 10 Haydn category – even very experienced teachers will find that one a challenge – but if you can consistently achieve a level 6 or above, you will be showing that you are in charge and be delivering lessons that you feel are competent and good learning experiences for the pupils.

Below are some ideas you might like to consider as good class-room management practice:

- Always be prepared – ensure thorough lesson planning and that you have access to resources and equipment, preferably before the lesson starts.

- Insist on common courtesies from the pupils – pupils putting hands up to ask questions, reminding them to say 'please' and 'thank you', being courteous to everyone in the room.

- Avoid shouting – use your voice as a tool not a weapon. Aim to address a class in a normal conversational tone and volume.

- Insist that all pupils remain seated and that there is no unnecessary movement around the room.

- Do not sit down at the teacher's desk for long periods in the lesson; move around the room monitoring what is going on and offering help.

- Establish a business-like atmosphere in the room from the start.

- Do not make threats or promises that you can't carry out.

- Stick to the rules – have a copy of the school's code of conduct and rewards and sanctions policy to refer to if needed.

- Don't be afraid to send for help if you are in a situation that is beyond your ability or experience to cope with.

- Record all misdemeanours for the HoD (or whoever the immediate line manager is) and the absent teacher and follow up on any major breaches of discipline before the end of the day.

- If the school has a pro forma to record breaches of discipline, fill it out with the relevant details as soon as you can.

- Humour is often a good way to defuse situations that might be getting out of hand.

- Be firm but fair – don't forget to reward pupils as well as to sanction them.

- Never make deals or negotiate with pupils just to placate them. Take a stand and keep to it, as long as it is within school guidelines.

- Don't be afraid to adapt or amend a lesson mid-stream if you think it is going badly, making sure, of course, that what you substitute is going to be in line with the lesson objectives and learning outcomes.

- Carry enough basic equipment with you to save spending time looking for pens and pencils, etc.

- Think about how to address your class or individuals. 'We'd all appreciate it if you would work more quietly' is better than a bellowed 'Shut up!'

- Always have a number of supplementary and extension activities at hand for those who finish their work before the end of the lesson.

- When addressing the whole class, insist on total silence and their full attention before speaking. The same applies when a pupil is speaking to the whole class.

Not all of these will work all of the time. Classroom management and disciplinary matters are not exact sciences. There is no magic wand! As a supply teacher you can only do your best in the circumstances that you are in. Good schools will support you. Those that don't, keep away from!

When classroom management works well and you have had a series of successful, pleasant lessons, you will want to return to the school on another assignment. But if all has not gone well, what do you do?

First, avoid falling into the trap of assuming that bad lessons are entirely your fault. If you have done your planning adequately and all other aspects of the lesson were in place, then you have nothing to reproach yourself for. Teachers are the worst people in the world for taking the blame for everything that happens in the classroom.

So-called bad lessons can be caused by a multitude of circumstances, some of which might well be beyond your control. Such things as:

- poor weather conditions – wet and windy days cause some pupils to get a bit frisky and silly;
- the unannounced (or unknown by you as a supply teacher) fire practice;
- constant interruptions by pupils or staff;
- failure of technology – computers, data projectors and the like;
- loss of pupils' books or the inability of the supply teacher to locate them;
- locked cupboards (and the key in the possession of the absent teacher) that contain vital resources for your lesson;
- a stream of late-comers – some might have legitimate reasons; most won't;
- other staff, usually the more senior ones, requesting individuals or groups of pupils to be taken out of your lesson for some reason.

Even insults hurled at you by pupils are rarely meant to be taken personally. You can't solve every problem that pupils have, and you shouldn't try to, especially if your only contact with them is the hour-long lesson. Experience tells me that the rude and irritating pupil you've just experienced is also the rude and irritating pupil that the other members of staff come across every single day. It's strangely comforting to know others face the same problems as you.

Second, avoid what Dave Stott, a former headteacher of 30 years' experience, calls the 'emotional highjack', being suddenly wrongfooted by a pupil's bad behaviour and finding yourself wondering what to do about it. He suggests a number of strategies that can help you through the stressful periods when your self-esteem and confidence are draining away through that massive hole in your emotional dam.

I've summarised his suggestions below:

- Take a moment before reacting to establish your own response, both verbal and non-verbal.

- Your reaction will be determined by how you feel and what has happened to you during the day, at home as well as at work. Spend time creating your teaching and learning environment and being aware of the pressures on you from elsewhere.

- Practise self-calming techniques: deep breathing, counting to 10, the internal monologue to assess and rehearse your response, seeing the 'bigger picture' and not feeling the compulsion to get involved and solve everyone's problems.

- Body language – how you stand and what you do with your hands (in front of you, palms down and unclenched); are you face to face with the pupil or slightly side on? Is your stance threatening, or calming but assertive?

- Verbal responses – avoid asking questions that could lead to an aggressive argument; give clear and precise instructions in a calm but assertive voice; avoid threats which pupils will immediately seize upon and challenge you to carry out.

In any confrontational situation it is you who must be in command of the situation, not the other way round. It is you who should be calm, but in control. Use other adults in the room and don't be afraid of asking for help if necessary. It is not a sign of weakness to request the HoD or other senior staff for assistance in confrontational situations.

↗ brilliant case study

The following situation actually happened to me while working as a supply teacher.

I'd been at the school for some time and knew the place and people well. I'd been forewarned by the cover manager that I would probably be covering this lesson the next day. It was Year 10 Design and Technology, double period (two hours) on a Wednesday morning. Like animals and birds can detect an on-coming storm, supply teachers develop a sixth sense about certain classes. I'd covered this teacher's groups before and knew what to expect. He had two Year 10 groups – one, a pleasant and hardworking group, the other came under the '… challenging pupils, but I'm sure you'll cope' banner. Of course I ended up with that one!

The routine was that cover work was left on a table in the staffroom. If it were a planned absence, the work was usually placed there the night before. For unplanned absences, the work usually appeared between 8 and 8.30 a.m. It was 8.40 and there was no sign of any work on the table. I asked the cover manager what had happened and was told that the absent teacher was writing the work in his office. He was the head of a one-man department and also a head of house.

He had forgotten that he had to go to a meeting that day and had not planned any work. I found his office and he was writing the cover work on the school's pro forma. My sense of doom was increased when he said, 'I don't know what to give these kids today.'

I suggested he'd better hurry up and find something as the lesson was due to start in 15 minutes. He hurriedly scribbled something down and handed it to me. 'That'll do for them,' he said. I had trouble interpreting his handwriting, but finally made sense of the lesson 'plan'. I knew at that point that there was not enough for two hours' work. 'They're slow workers,' he said. 'Anyway, they'll be a TA with you.'

I reached his classroom at 8.50 and wrote the lesson notes on the whiteboard, got out the books and paper and waited for the storm to

▷

break. I had no seating plan, but eventually found a register under a pile of papers. One by one, they arrived. I stood at the door and greeted them as usual, with a smile and a 'good morning'. Some responded, others ignored me and several greeted me with, 'Are we having you today?' I resisted giving the obvious answer!

I asked them to sit in their usual seats and to take outdoor coats off. I called the register – it took nearly five minutes – and attempted to explain the lesson to them. They were not interested. 'Why can't we do practical work?' several shouted out. I explained that Mr X wanted them to do this work and he had not left any instructions to the contrary.

That didn't work either. At 9.15 some had started to work, but the promised TA was nowhere to be seen. He arrived a few minutes later and my spirits rose slightly as there would at least be another adult with me. However, he told me he wouldn't be in that lesson as he had other things to do. He left and didn't return! This too unsettled the pupils and a lot of chatter started up. Little or no work was being done by the majority.

This was not looking good! Then, without warning or preamble, something happened that I'd never experienced in over 30 years of teaching – an outbreak of coughing. It started slowly and spread around the room like a bush fire. Nearly everyone had suddenly developed a rasping cough. It went on for several minutes like a chorus from hell and at first I treated it as a joke. I made one or two humorous quips but it made no difference. I asked for quiet, reminded them about good manners and courtesy but to no avail. After a few minutes of this cacophony and having tried a number of tactics, I decided I had only one sensible choice to make. I asked one of the girls, who was looking embarrassed at the idiocy of her classmates, to go and fetch the head. There was almost instantaneous silence. The coughing miraculously stopped. Work, of a sort, was being done. It was too late to stop the girl and I waited for the head to appear.

Within minutes he came to the room. I told him what had happened and several pupils admitted to starting the outbreak of coughing. He took them away for the rest of the lesson and read the riot act to the others.

The lesson proceeded, but many of the pupils had finished the work by the end of the first period. Only an hour to go!

As I had no extension work for them and it was a subject that I could not really help them with, I suggested that if they had any coursework to finish, that they could do so. Failing that any work from another subject or unfinished homework could be done. A few took up the suggestion and got on with it. Most asked if they could do practical work.

I had a decision to make. It was a calculated risk, but I said that if they had work to complete in the workshop that they could do it. Fortunately, the workshop was next door to the room, linked by an adjoining door. So, like the mythical two-headed Janus, I stood between two classrooms, one eye on the group doing written work, the other on the chisel and hammer brigade. It could have been an unmitigated disaster, but it worked. I even managed to help some of them, showing them how to hold a saw and quoted my father who always told me, 'Let the saw do the work, not you.' The second lesson passed without incident.

At the end of the second period as they were leaving for break, some of them came up to me and apologised for their appalling behaviour. I accepted their apology and asked them why they had done it. 'You're the third supply teacher we've had this week, sir,' they said. 'We never see Mr X any more.'

When lunchtime came and the dust had settled I sat and analysed the lesson from hell. What could be learnt from it? Well, a number of things emerged:

- I was still in one piece and they hadn't attacked me with sharpened chisels and Stanley knives.
- I had kept calm, taken several deep breaths and thought through my strategy and responses.
- I had taken a calculated risk and changed the lesson plan mid-stream.
- The coughing episode wasn't aimed at me personally, but it was more an expression of the frustration the pupils felt at a system which they perceived had let them down.

▶

- I reminded myself that it is not a sign of weakness to ask for help.
- Some of the pupils had shown moral courage and respect in apologising at the end of the lesson.
- I reminded myself that nothing that had happened in a negative way was a result of anything I had done – an important self-confidence boost, if nothing else. It was the result of poor planning and indifference by the regular teacher to the situation I had been put in, and a TA who apparently found more interesting things to do.

It was by far the worst lesson I'd taught for many years, but maintaining control over the situation enabled me and the pupils to salvage something from it. Needless to say I followed up the problems I had encountered with the head and the teacher and filled out the relevant disciplinary forms.

At least I went away from that lesson knowing that most of the pupils had achieved a positive outcome of sorts, even if it was not what the teacher originally envisaged.

Personal survival kit

One of the major disadvantages of being a supply teacher is that you end up carrying your 'office' with you from place to place. This personal survival kit, as some call it, can become burdensome if you let it, so below is a list of what I consider to be the essentials for both primary and secondary assignments.

- good sized bag to carry everything;
- stock of pencils (at least 20) and some pens;
- several rulers and erasers;
- pencil sharpener;
- an A4 pad of lined paper and some plain paper;
- a ring binder folder in which to keep lesson notes and essential paperwork, etc.;

- several whiteboard marker pens (a range of colours is useful);
- an academic diary or planner with term dates and holidays.

Some supply teachers always carry a memory stick with lesson ideas and so on.

brilliant tip

A word of warning – school computer systems are notorious for getting viruses and I have had several memory sticks corrupted this way. Have a 'clean' memory stick in hand.

It's possible that at some time you will be covering a PE lesson, especially in a secondary school, so it's worth carrying a track suit, a pair of trainers and a whistle (do you really want to borrow one from the PE department?) and leave them in the car until needed. If you are asked to take PE in a primary school, I would certainly suggest that a pair of trainers is essential for indoor or outdoor activities.

Other essentials are:

- your own mug;
- a stock of tea bags or sachets of coffee and sugar;
- a few snacks;
- an up-to-date A to Z or SatNav;
- a number of lesson ideas, especially starter activities (quizzes, word searches, word or number games, etc.) which can be easily photocopied.

And don't forget to leave room for the plethora of paperwork you might be given when you start a new assignment (code of conduct, policy documents, school map and so on).

brilliant recap

- As a supply teacher you will have a lack of permanency in your daily work but that should not stop you from treating the assignment as if it's your full-time job.

- No matter how long or short a time you are in a school, you are in charge of the classroom and everything that goes on in it.

- Create a business-like atmosphere in your classroom from the start.

- Classroom management is about people, time, resources and the physical space.

- Set out your expectations of the pupils at the start of each lesson.

- Where possible, get to the classroom before the pupils and be ready for them with a greeting and with information on the board about the lesson.

- Keep to the rules of the school – always.

- Stay calm and in control – practise your classroom management skills.

- Follow up on any breaches of discipline.

- Be prepared by carrying some essential items with you.

CHAPTER 8

'Would you mind leaving the staffroom …?'

By now it should be fairly obvious what makes a good supply teacher and a good school to work in as a supply teacher. However, it wouldn't be a bad idea to revisit one or two points and to look at a few experiences of supply teachers out there in the field, the people who are at the sharp end of agency practices and schools' attitudes to 'the supply teacher'.

The experiences of many supply staff are less than positive in far too many cases, but that is not to say that there aren't some good schools out there and some honourable recruitment agencies that look after their clients properly.

Let me start by reviewing some aspects of good practice before going on to look at what I consider to be a model and exemplary school and then one that falls below the standards we should expect from fellow professionals.

The brilliant school

What constitutes a good school to work in as a supply teacher? Let me reiterate what I consider to be a school that I would be happy to be a part of:

- a warm greeting on arrival;
- given a 'welcome pack' with all the essential information that I will need;
- a map of the school;

- a tour of the school by the cover manager or a designated person (some schools use pupils for this);

- a clear indication of what the assignment entails – subject(s) to be covered, ability of pupils, etc.;

- a timetable with lessons, timings (including lunch and break times);

- other duties expected of the supply teacher, such as break and lunch duties, after school duties, assemblies and meetings;

- emergency contact names and internal phone numbers;

- registration procedures, assembly rota;

- policies on rewards/sanctions, disciplinary matters, toilet visits by pupils during lessons;

- class lists, seating plans for classes to be covered;

- access to ICT, photocopiers, temporary log-in details;

- procedures for booking ICT rooms, library and other non-classroom facilities;

- introduction to key staff – HoD, deputy head, pastoral heads;

- involvement in INSET/CPD courses;

- effective and regular monitoring of your performance in the classroom.

I should say at this point that not all of these need to be given to the supply teacher on the first morning. Some will be provided by the cover manager; others by HoD or other staff within the first few days of a medium- or long-term assignment.

For a short-term assignment, it is obvious that some of the points above will not be relevant at all. It might also be up to the supply teacher to ask for some of the information. Schools are busy places and not everybody has time to see to the needs of the supply teacher without some prompting occasionally.

Make your requirements known, but don't make a pest of yourself if you don't get them met straight away!

The brilliant supply teacher

Schools are only half of the equation. The supply teacher also has responsibilities. Below are what I consider the qualities of a good supply teacher and one whom I would be happy to employ:

- being on time particularly on the first day;
- having some basic equipment – some emergency lesson plans, a stock of pens and pencils, A4 paper, diary/planner, etc.;
- prepared to go 'the extra mile';
- consistent in the treatment of pupil and colleagues;
- carrying out procedures in accordance with school policies and rules;
- respecting departmental or school facilities and resources;
- being polite and friendly to pupils and staff;
- becoming a 'member of staff' as quickly as possible if on long-term assignment;
- showing competence in the classroom, with expert subject specialism knowledge, or ability to be as involved as possible in other subjects if on general cover;
- flexible in approach to work assignments;
- willing to travel and take last-minute assignment requests from agencies, or last-minute changes at the school;
- being well prepared for lessons with competent lesson planning evident;
- effective classroom management and discipline;

- showing ability to make own decisions without having to ask others constantly, but also having the good sense to ask for help if it's needed.

Of course, not every school or individual supply teacher can necessarily fulfil all the criteria outlined above. Supply teachers, however, should expect the majority of them to apply, depending on the type of school or institution and the nature and length of the assignment. There's no reason a school cannot make a supply teacher feel welcome and provide them with some basic necessities even if the teacher is there for only a day or two.

Similarly, the supply teacher should approach each assignment, regardless of the type or length, with professionalism and enthusiasm. As the saying goes, you only have one chance to make a good first impression! A sure way to get return work is to leave your mark in as many positive ways as possible.

And what about agencies? Look at any agency booklet or brochure and you will get the impression that this agency is 'the one for you'. Full of happy, contented, bright-eyed, usually young supply teachers in front of smiling, well-behaved, enthusiastic pupils, you might think that supply teaching is the perfect job.

Agencies, especially the bigger, nationally recognised ones, spend a lot of time, creative energy, resources and money fostering that impression and attracting their clients – you, the supply teacher. They will proudly trumpet that they have the government's Quality Mark, but just how reliable is that when you are assessing the agency's overall worth and performance?

Let's not forget – agencies are businesses and the *raison d'être* of any business is to make a profit. That in itself is not a bad thing, but the welfare of the client also has to be part of their service. You've only to look at a few teachers' forums to find that not all agencies live up to their glossy image and that not all supply teachers are happy with the treatment they receive from their agency.

Consider how you are treated from the start of your relationship with an agency. A warm welcome from helpful and friendly staff is a good beginning. But how long does that feeling last? Is the agency giving you regular work? Are your skills and experiences being fully recognised in the types of assignments you are offered? Does the agency pay you on time? Do you feel exploited and undervalued by your agency? Are any problems and queries you have dealt with promptly by the staff? Do they offer you any training, CPD courses, refresher courses and so on? Is there proper monitoring of your performance by the agency as well as by the school?

It should be stated as well that many of the teaching unions have 'severe reservations [about agencies] as many agencies undercut national pay rates and conditions of service applicable to teachers employed directly by local authorities or schools' (*Supply Teachers: Pay, Conditions and Working Time*, NUT, 2010).

The area of pay is perhaps the most contentious among supply teachers, but other exploitative practices by agencies cannot be ignored, such as sending a qualified, experienced teacher to an assignment that turns out to be nothing more than a cover supervisor role. *Caveat emptor!*

Many supply teachers will have a store of horror stories to tell about schools and agencies. Equally, many will be very satisfied with the work they receive and the means of getting it. As with most aspects of work, there are always two sides to every story. As a supply teacher you have to play your part in getting the best out of whatever situation you find yourself in, even if the school does not necessarily play its part to the full.

Teachers who refuse to be flexible in their attitudes or who constantly grumble about the conditions they face are unlikely to be well received if they ever secure a return assignment. In fact, they might never receive a return assignment!

The same applies to a supply teacher who arrives late without any equipment of their own and expects the school to do everything for them, expecting simply to stand in front of a class without having to do anything else. These are extreme examples, as I hope you will realise, and in the years I have been a full-time teacher, as well as a supply teacher, I have only come across a handful who fall into this category.

Just as schools and agencies keep records of supply teachers they regard as inefficient or incompetent, so you might feel like keeping records of schools that you wish to avoid or return to.

brilliant tip

A supply colleague of mine keeps a 'black book' of all the schools he works in and grades each school with comments in a quasi-Ofsted way. Perhaps the following headings will be useful if you decide to do this:

- welcome and induction process;
- staff support;
- overall atmosphere of the school;
- pupil behaviour ...

... with a simple A–G or 1–10 mark for each category!

As we saw in the case studies in Chapter 1, some supply teachers are inefficient, incompetent or just simply wrong for the job. These do not last long in supply teaching. But what about schools that don't come up to the mark?

In the course of preparing this book, I interviewed a number of supply colleagues and recorded their experiences. Of all the interviews two stood out as worthy of special attention. The first one would probably receive an F or G on the above grading system; the second I would consider to be a model school in the way it deals with supply staff on every level, from initial booking to the time they leave at the end of their assignment. It should be noted that no schools or staff are indentified by name or detailed location.

brilliant case study

Secondary School 11–16 – West Midlands
Assignment – short-term (2–3 days) science cover

The female supply teacher had been contacted quite late by her agency (largely because the school had been late informing the agency) and had done her best to get to the school on time despite the fact that she was not sure where the school was located.

When she arrived there was no-one to meet her. She signed in, was handed a visitors' badge and told to wait in reception until someone came for her. Several minutes later a pupil came to reception on an errand and was told by the receptionist to take the supply teacher to where she would be teaching. There was no tour of the school or induction pack offered. The pupil escorted her to the science department and she arrived at her classroom five minutes before the class, who were on their way from an assembly.

The HoD escorted the class in – a Year 11 Set 3 group – and settled them, telling them what work had been set. He didn't introduce himself to the supply teacher or her to the class. She did this herself later on in the lesson when there was suitable pause in the noise. She was, as expected, bombarded with the usual questions: Who are you? Are you another supply teacher? Where was sir?

Little work was achieved in that lesson, she told me. The work consisted of copying great chunks of a text book, accompanied by a few drawings. The class was noisy and she had problems getting their attention. Overall, she said, they showed little or no interest in the 'mindless task'. As an experienced and well-qualified science teacher, she felt utterly dispirited by what she had to do. She said, 'I tried to inject a bit of my own knowledge in the lesson, but it was a waste of time.' At the end of the lesson one of the pupils came up to her and said, 'Don't worry, miss. It's always like that!'

Period two was a free so she tried to prepare some work for the next class, a Year 9 group. She couldn't find anyone who could tell her where the appropriate text books were kept as this wasn't made clear on the brief lesson notes left for her by the HoD.

In the staffroom at break, she asked about getting a drink and was told to help herself if she could find a mug. Fortunately, being an experienced supply teacher, she had bought her own mug and some coffee. By the time she had managed to get to the kettle, however, break was nearly over. Nobody bothered to speak to me, she said. 'I might just as well have been invisible for all the notice anyone took of me.'

Before going to break she had put some notes on the whiteboard for the next period, but when she returned to the classroom she found much of it had been rubbed off or defaced by pupils who had been in the classroom, against all the rules, during break.

This sort of behaviour by pupils and staff set the tone for the rest of the day – unruly pupils and unconcerned staff.

On the positive side, the HoD popped his head round the door several times to see if everything was all right and then promptly left. She had a few run-ins with several pupils who point blank refused to do as asked during her lessons. One of them said, 'All we have these days is supply teachers.' She said, 'I nearly told them I'm not surprised if this is how you behave, but thought better of it. He was bigger than me!'

During lunch the HoD came up to her and had a chat. He apologised for not being around much in the morning, but he had his own classes to teach. He told her not to worry about teaching them too much. 'All I want for the next two days is a hot body in front of the classes to prevent chaos from breaking out.' In other words, she told me, I was doing no more than crowd control. 'Why did I spend four years at university to end up doing this?' she asked. I had no reply.

During the changeover from one afternoon period to another, she had to break up a fight between two pupils on the stairs just outside her room. She reported this to the HoD and was told he would deal with it. She heard nothing more of the incident from the HoD or any senior staff.

On the second day things were much the same. However, after lunch on that day, the head wanted a short staff meeting that would impinge on the first 10 minutes or so of the first afternoon period. The supply teacher was sitting in the staffroom when the head walked in. He saw her and headed in her direction. He said, 'You're the supply, aren't you? Would you mind leaving the staffroom as you aren't a member of staff and are not needed in the meeting?' No explanation was given as to why she wasn't required in the meeting or any chance given to absent herself voluntarily out of consideration for any confidential matters that might have been discussed in the meeting.

She left feeling demeaned and totally undervalued.

On her way out at the end of the assignment she reflected on the school and her experience there. She said, 'I was still in one piece; had not been attacked by any pupils; some work had been achieved (a nice little Year 7 group apparently); and I'd managed to prevent two pupils from killing each other on the stairs.' Those were the plus points!

On the negative side the school had almost totally ignored her and had offered no support or encouragement. The work was undemanding and derivative which led to very little engagement by the pupils. For reasons she never found out, the absent teacher had not left any work.

When she got into her car she realised that at no time during her two days there had she been introduced to the cover manager – the very person who had rung the agency to start with and had requested a supply teacher!

She told me afterwards that when she first entered the school there was an atmosphere of hostility and tension. She formed the distinct impression that morale was low and when she looked up the school's last Ofsted report she ▶

could see why. It had gained a 'Satisfactory' overall grading. Damned with faint praise, in other words!

Contrast the attitude of that school with this one.

⌐ brilliant case study

Secondary school 11–18 – Warwickshire
Assignment – English cover (medium to long-term)

As this assignment was going to last at least a few weeks, perhaps even extending to a term, the supply teacher visited the school the day before the assignment was due to begin. He told me that as soon as he walked into the school he could feel a friendly and welcoming atmosphere. The reception area was colourful and had displays and information that immediately gave the impression of a school that was proud of itself.

He was met initially by two pupil receptionists who signed him in and gave him a visitor's badge. They informed the school's receptionist that he had arrived and she then rang for the cover manager.

The cover manager came down to reception a short time after and greeted the supply teacher. He gave him an 'introductory pack' with some basic information that the supply teacher would need during his first few days. Unlike most schools, where the cover manager is more likely to be a senior member of staff, this school had appointed a non-teaching member of staff to that position.

Anyone who has worked in a busy secondary school knows that first thing in the morning most senior staff are run off their feet with all manner of tasks that need to be done urgently before the teaching day begins. To get hold of a senior member of staff at that time of day is difficult enough; holding their attention long enough to settle in a new member of staff is impossible.

The supply teacher was taken to the staffroom and given a cup of coffee. He had a preliminary chat with the cover manager who explained the nature of the assignment. The supply teacher was told that it would certainly last several weeks, but that there was the possibility that it would go on for a lot longer. That was, in fact, what happened.

After the chat, the cover manager took him on a tour of the school and introduced him to the key members of the department in which he would work. The HoD, who was available at this point, took over and showed him the resources, stockroom, the room in which he would be teaching and so on. He gave him class registers, the absent teacher's timetable and planner, seating plans and a school diary. The supply teacher was allowed to spend some time in his new classroom familiarising himself with his environment while the pupils were at an assembly.

He was told by the HoD that if he wanted anything or had any queries that he should ask any member of the department or the cover manager at any time. The HoD also told him that he would be monitored for the first few days to make sure that everything was running smoothly.

Because the supply teacher had gone in the day before he was due to start the assignment, he could use the majority of that day to prepare lessons and find his way around the school. He visited the library and introduced himself to the librarian; checked out the ICT facilities (within a few days he'd been given temporary log-in facilities); familiarised himself with the routines and practices of the school, particularly the rules about discipline, rewards and sanctions and general expectations about pupil behaviour in and out of the classroom. He said, 'It was clear from the start that it was a school that had high expectations of everyone who worked there. There was a very positive atmosphere and eagerness to succeed. I was told by one member of staff that the school had been through some difficult times and for a long time had had a poor reputation. All that had changed now and the school was well regarded in the community.'

Throughout his assignment he was treated as a full-time member of staff and was supported by the department and the senior staff at all times. He attended parents' evenings (despite having a 45 minute journey home at the end of them); school CPD sessions; department and staff meetings, and ▶

the daily full-staff briefing meeting; and took part in helping to prepare a school drama production.

Over the course of the first few days, the cover manager made it his business to check that all was going well and to sort out any problems that the supply teacher might have.

During my interview with him he said that, in his opinion, a supply teacher should 'create a positive feeling and environment ...' and that 'the supply teacher makes the running and should go "the extra mile" '.

The assignment lasted several terms and the supply teacher became *de facto* a full member of staff. He showed himself to be competent, enthusiastic and flexible, and was popular with the pupils. The department was highly satisfied with him and he appreciated all the support and encouragement he received from them.

When the teacher whom he was covering returned, he acted in a support role for a while until the teacher could take up the reins again with confidence.

When he left the assignment, he was thanked by the head and given a farewell card signed by the staff at the end of one of the daily briefing meetings.

As a postscript to this case study, a full-time post became available at the school a few weeks after his supply contract had finished and the supply teacher in question applied for it and was given the job. The fact that he was known, trusted and had proved himself a competent and experienced teacher at the school must have been greatly in his favour.

Two schools of similar profiles, intake and setting, but with radically different approaches and attitudes to their supply staff!

What you never hear a supply teacher say

And finally, a somewhat tongue-in-cheek section – What you never hear a supply teacher say – courtesy of the *TES Connect* forum:

- 'Thanks for setting them the "design a poster" lesson. It's one of my favourites!'
- 'No, I'm not a proper teacher.'
- 'I love my agency.'
- 'I think you are paying me too much.'
- 'Of course I'll go outside on duty. I love freezing to death and standing out in the rain, wind, hurricane, blizzard!'
- 'Yes it was me who designed this c**p cover lesson.'
- 'I'd love a coffee, thanks. The leprosy has nearly cleared up now.'
- Feedback to teacher: 'The children thoroughly enjoyed copying from the textbook and were fully engaged and on task the whole lesson.'
- And one that will resonate with many, I suspect: 'This thread has reminded me of the very non-humorous aspects of supply. The utter gnawing misery of struggling financially, being treated like a sub-slave by the agency, a non-person by the school staff and oddly enough, probably the best of all by the students, the uphill struggle and personal doubts of applying for jobs, the grim grit of cracking on and getting in there with a smile and a positive attitude, being the professional whilst feeling like a devalued, second-rate cast off. I hope I never feel like that again. The baffling fact was that I chose all of that ... mad.'

brilliant recap

- A good supply teacher is flexible, positive, enthusiastic and professional ... despite what the school or agency might throw at them.

- Schools that value their supply staff look after them from the moment of arrival to the day they finish their assignment.

- The role of agencies is vital in ensuring that the school and the supply teacher get the best out of each other.

- As a supply teacher be prepared to say no to assignments that you feel are unsuitable for you.

- Choose your agency with care.

- Always tell your agency if there are problems at the schools you are sent to.

CHAPTER 9

The future of supply teaching

The future of supply teaching is inextricably tied into the future of education in the UK and, without doubt, the current state of our education system is more uncertain now than it has been in the past 30 years. It has gone through numerous changes in that time, but the majority of them have been curricula changes – the introduction of GCSE and SATs, for instance – rather than wholesale structural changes to the very fabric of education that we are seeing now.

As a result many teachers are feeling a great sense of trepidation and uncertainty about the future. Schools are facing budget cuts and students at post-16 level have had their Education Maintenance Allowance (EMA) scrapped which could lead to fewer students staying on in education. The problem surrounding university funding has, of course, been well-documented and needs no elaboration here.

The situation regarding education funding is perhaps best summed up by the University and College Union Congress in May 2011: 'The UK could become yesterday's country equipped with yesterday's skills if education cuts continue …'

In a poll of 1177 school and college leaders it is suggested that 'more than half of the schools in England are facing cuts to their budgets' (BBC News, May 2011).

Add to these the seemingly relentless march towards academy status for many schools, the introduction of the so-called Free

Schools, problems with pensions and working conditions and it is little wonder that the profession is in a state of flux, confusion, fear and uncertainty. At the time of writing, a number of these problems and uncertainties have yet to be resolved and it might be some time before we see the full effects of the changes.

Where does all this leave the supply teacher? A number of the changes that I have mentioned briefly will directly affect your role as a supply teacher. Others will have an indirect effect and it is worth exploring these issues if only to be aware of their importance and impact. However, not all of them are negative, as we will see.

Introduction of cover supervisors

Cover supervisors are a relatively recent addition to schools and came about as a result of the 'Remodelling of the School Workforce' agenda in 2005, and with the introduction of 'rarely cover' in 2009. Originally they were intended to give a few days' cover for absent colleagues before a supply teacher was brought in if the cover were to last longer than the two or three days.

Cover supervisors are not qualified teachers and often work alongside TAs in the classroom. However, some schools are now using cover supervisors as substitutes for supply teachers – as they are also doing with TAs – at least for short-term cover arrangements. Some agencies are also sending qualified supply teachers on cover supervisor assignments. The effect of this is to undermine the position of the supply teacher in schools which could in turn compromise the education of pupils.

Let's not forget that cover supervisors cost approximately half what a school would pay for a supply teacher. It is to be expected, therefore, that in times of budget cuts, schools will opt for the least expensive way of covering absent colleagues.

The role of cover supervisors in schools is important, but they should be used in the way they were intended, not as a substitute for qualified, experienced supply teachers.

Academies

Academies were introduced under the last Labour administration as a way of rebranding and turning around failing schools. The present coalition government has taken this forward and is now extending academy status to many secondary schools.

To date over 1000 schools have applied for academy status since June 2010 and a third of all secondary schools are now academies (DfE website information, June 2011).

As we have seen previously, these independent, state funded schools do not have to adhere to national agreements on pay or working conditions. Academies could, if they wish, revoke the 'rarely cover' agreement and use internal staff for cover, thus depriving supply teachers of work opportunities.

brilliant tip

Before accepting an assignment in an academy, especially if it's a medium- to long-term one, check on the following:

- working hours, length of the working day (including if staff are asked to work during holidays);
- pay rates, especially if you are employed directly by the school or LA;
- whether PPA is safeguarded time;
- if there is additional working time outside the contractual working time;
- the practice regarding attendance at meetings;
- professional development arrangements.

Unfortunately there is little or no documentation on the position of supply teachers in academies so it is difficult to assess the impact academies could have on them. It's a case of forewarned is forearmed.

Free schools

In September 2011 the first twenty-four free schools opened their doors for the first time to pupils.

As with academies, these are independent, state funded schools in both the primary and secondary sectors and can be set up by 'charities, universities, businesses, education groups, *visionary teachers or committed parents*' [my italics] (DfE website information).

It would seem that in many ways they are academies by any other name. However, the most worrying aspect of them from a teacher's point of view is their policy on employing staff. The following is a quotation from the DfE:

'*Free Schools* do not have to employ teachers with Qualified Teacher Status *(although certain specialist posts will still require QTS). Instead, Free Schools have the freedom to appoint the people they believe are best equipped to deliver their unique educational vision, for example an experienced instructor or lecturer from a further education institution. Ensuring the highest quality of teaching is paramount to the success of each school' (my italics).*

Source: DfE, **www.education.gov.uk**

Michael Gove, the Secretary of State for Education said, '... we will not be setting overly prescriptive requirements in relation to qualifications ...' (response to a question in the House of Commons, November 2010).

If they do not have to employ qualified full-time teachers, where does that leave supply teachers if they are required in a free school? Presumably the policy will be that anyone can stand in front of a group of pupils and teach them!

Needless to say, the main teaching unions have something to say about this. The NASUWT argues that 'using staff without QTS in the wrong circumstances is an abuse ...'. Likewise, the NUT states that 'people are perfectly aware that if unqualified teachers become the norm in free schools it will simply be to cut costs'.

I suppose a group of supply teachers could get together and open a free school. At least the pupils would have qualified and experienced staff!

As with academies, at present there is no documentation specific to supply teachers and their role in free schools.

Pensions

The position of supply teachers and pensions is variable. If you work through an agency or have opted out of the Teachers' Pension Scheme (TPS) then you are not affected by the coming changes to public sector pensions. However, if you still contribute to the TPS then you might well be affected. Supply teachers who are now retired from full-time teaching and in receipt of a pension, of course, will not be affected by these changes and will continue to receive their pension as normal. Currently this is one of the biggest threats to the teaching profession and could lead to industrial action.

Without going into great detail, if you still contribute to the TPS you will be paying more, working longer and receiving less when you retire. The coalition government is moving away from final salary to 'career average pay'. The suggestion is that teachers will receive 1/100 of career average pay for every year in teaching. This compares to the current system of 1/60 final pay or 1/80 final pay plus a lump sum. One union estimates that retired teachers could lose up to £10,000 a year under these new proposals!

On a more positive note ...

Paternity leave

Supply teachers will be familiar with covering maternity leave, but as of April 2011 paternity leave will be extended to 26 weeks on top of the statutory 2 weeks allowed now. Another small window of opportunity for supply staff?

One-to-one tuition

This is another relatively new post in many schools that could provide employment opportunities for supply teachers. The scheme was originally set up to enable schools, both primary and secondary, to offer individualised tuition to pupils struggling with maths and English to bring them up to national standards. The qualifications to become a one-to-one tutor (based on DfE website information) are:

- someone with QTS;
- an overseas qualified teacher eligible to teach in UK schools;
- NQTs in the summer before they attain QTS;
- those with teaching experience in FE or HE sectors.

Some schools will conduct one-to-one sessions during normal school hours, while others will fit it in before or after school or even during holidays or weekends.

Agency Workers' Regulations 2010

This is a major new piece of employment legislation, stemming from the EU Temporary Workers' Directive 2008, and came into force in the UK on 1 October 2011.

Essentially, it guarantees agency workers equal treatment, alongside their full-time colleagues, regarding pay and working conditions.

In order to qualify for this the agency worker will have to complete 'twelve weeks service in the *same* role with the *same* hirer' (my italics). What the phrase 'same role' means is not clearly defined at this stage. Is a supply teacher hired to cover, say, English, in a different role if they return to the same school to cover art?

However, these 12 weeks do *not* have to be consecutive and you 'can accrue [them] over a much longer period of work and through more than one agency'. The entitlements include pay, duration of working time, rest periods, rest breaks and annual leave.

There is also what is called 'Day One Rights'. These apply from the first day of an assignment and state that:

- hirers must inform agency workers of existing vacancies in their organisations;
- agency workers will be entitled to access 'collective on-site facilities such as crêche and childcare facilities, canteens, car parking ...'.

Pregnant agency workers will also be entitled to paid time off to attend medical appointments and antenatal classes but only *when they have achieved the 12 weeks' qualifying service.*

A new qualifying period will come into force if a new assignment with the same hirer is substantively different or if there is more than a six-week break between assignments.

The qualifying period will be paused (not stopped) if the agency worker takes:

- a break of six weeks or fewer;

- certified sick leave for no more than 28 weeks;
- statutory maternity/paternity leave;
- time off for public duty, such as jury service.

The future

While it seems that education is all doom and gloom at the moment, there will always be a need for supply teachers. Supply staff perform a very valuable service in maintaining continuity of learning for pupils whose regular teacher is absent for one reason or another. The truth is that schools could not function properly when their staff are absent if it were not for supply teachers.

There are, without doubt, big challenges ahead. It is likely, for example, that we will see short-term supply work almost disappear, or at least become a rarity, as a result of the introduction of cover supervisors. Medium- and long-term cover, however, will always require qualified and experienced staff – not withstanding the free school policy – who have the skills and knowledge required to maintain good order in the classroom and to be able to provide continuity of learning as far as possible for the pupils affected.

In order to make the best of the situations we will find ourselves in, I believe we need to be more selective in our choice of assignments and be prepared to say no to agencies if they do not perform to our expectations. We need to become more flexible in our approach to the job and be prepared to 'make the running' and 'go the extra mile' if need be. We also need to be more financially savvy when it comes to pay rates, pension provision and so on.

Supply teaching will always be a demanding, and at times a difficult job, but it is also ultimately satisfying and fulfilling if approached in a professional and organised way.

Remember, schools need us more than we need them!

brilliant recap

On the whole book!

If you can answer yes to all 20 questions below, then you are well on your way to becoming a brilliant supply teacher.

- Do you have Qualified Teacher Status?
- Are you registered with the General Teaching Council?
- Do you have a current CRB?
- Do you have a current and well-constructed CV?
- If you are an overseas trained teacher, do you know what the current UK regulations are about being employed as a supply teacher?
- Can you recognise the qualities of a good, efficient agency compared to a poor agency?
- Can you state what you should expect from an agency?
- Can you state what a good agency can expect from you?
- Are you fully prepared for all the uncertainties, vagaries and variations you will encounter as a supply teacher?
- Are you confident in your classroom management skills?
- Do you have a survival kit at the ready?
- Do you have a series of lessons, starters, plenaries and ideas at hand if work is not set by the school?
- Are you competent at using Word, PowerPoint, Excel, etc.?
- Can you use the internet with ease?
- Are you aware of the different work patterns, timetables, lesson structures, ethos between primary and secondary schools?
- Do you know what a school can realistically expect from its supply staff?

- Do you know what you can reasonably expect from a school?

- Do you possess a good road atlas or SatNav system?

- Are you prepared to take the early morning/Sunday night call from an agency for a school placement?

- When you've had a really good day/lesson or an absolute nightmare of a day/lesson, can you answer the question: why?

Bibliography

Dougherty, Martin (1998) *The Art of Surviving Supply Teaching*. David Fulton: London.

Haydn, Terry (2006) *Managing Pupil Behaviour – Key Issues in Teaching and Learning*. Routledge: Abingdon, Oxon.

Leach, Sue (2006) *How to be a Successful Secondary Teacher*. Continuum: London/New York.

Murphy, Julia (2006) *100 Ideas for Supply Teachers (Secondary Edition)*. Continuum: London/New York.

Overall, Lyn and Sangster, Margaret (2003) *Secondary Teacher's Handbook*. Continuum: London/New York.

Parry, Michael (2006) *100 Ideas for Primary Supply Teachers*. Continuum: London/New York.

Smith, Jim (2010) *The Lazy Teacher's Handbook*. Crown House Publishing: Carmarthen, Wales.

Wallace, Isabella and Kirkman, Leah (2007) *Pimp Your Lessons*. Continuum: London/New York.

Journals, articles, and reports

Borrows, Peter (2000) 'Teaching Science to Pupils with Special Needs', *School Science Review*, 81(296): 37 (full text available on-line).

Chitsabesan, Prathiba *et al.* (2006) 'Mental Health Needs of Young Offenders in Custody and in the Community', *British Journal of Psychiatry,* 188(6): 534–540 (full text available on-line).

Hurry, Jane and Brazier, Laura (2005) 'Education and Training for Young Offenders', *NRDC Reflect Magazine,* on-line issue 3.

Hurry, Jane *et al.* (2010) *Young People in the Classroom – the observation study.* Young Offenders Research Report 2010, Chapter 2, p15 (full text available on-line). Published by the National Research and Development Centre (NRDC).

Hutchings, Merryn *et al.* (2006) *The Recruitment, Deployment and Management of Supply Teachers in England.* Research Report No. 738 (full report available on-line). London Metropolitan University and University of Glasgow.

Williams, Michelle and Gersch, Irvine (2004) 'Teaching in Mainstream Schools and Special Schools: are the stresses similar or different?', *British Journal of Special Education,* 31(3): 157–162.

Miscellaneous documents

The Agency Workers (Amendment) Regulations (2011) (SI No. 1941).

Supply Teachers: Pay, Conditions & Working Time (2010) available at **www.teachers.org.uk**

'*Young people and custody*' (2011) available at **www.direct. gov.uk**

'*Schools' use of temporary teachers*' (2002) available at **www.ofsted.gov.uk**

'*Current working conditions and experiences* of supply teachers', survey conducted in January 2008, NASUWT, available at **www.nasuwt.org.uk**

Teachers' Pay and Conditions in Academies (2011) NUT. available at **www.teachers.org.uk/taxomy/term/1731**

School Libraries – A Right (2011) Chartered Institute of Library and Information Professionals.

Schools Need School Librarians (2007) Chartered Institute of Library and Information Professionals.

Index